"If you have a dog, or are considering bringing a dog into your home, *Being a Super Pet Parent* will transform your approach and bring you and your dog a lifetime of rich rewards. Donna's storytelling and personal sharing of not only her experiences, but her passion for elevating our relationships with our canine companions, is a game-changer for individuals and families who want a life filled with the love of dog."

—Nancy Herbst, M.Ed.; certified Healing Touch practitioner;
certified spiritual director; loving pet parent

"Donna Chicone is a dog person's best friend! She has a passion for dogs and embraces the joy of the human-animal bond. With incredible energy, she works to educate others on all aspects of not just having dogs, but of sharing our lives with them. She brings together people from all areas of the dog world – from dog shows and breeders to trainers and veterinarians – to offer complete information for the serious dog lover."

—Kate An Hunter, D.V.M., Carver Lake Veterinary Center

"Having been a pet parent in my adult life – first for fourteen years and then for fifteen – I found reassurance that I gave the best I knew at the time. Since selecting another puppy and reading your book, I feel like there is so much more to being a pet parent than I originally thought. I have always loved dogs, but I did not view their needs in the same way as I do now."

—Pat Wall, BSN, RN; 30-year pet parent

"Wait a second while I hug and kiss my dog, wipe away a few tears, and take my dog for a little adventure in nature so she can explore, smell, and run – that is the impact this book had on me ... not to mention I could not put it down! The book is very informative, easy to follow and read, makes a great deal of sense, follows sound logic, and is nicely sequential. This will be my gift of the season for all my dog-loving friends!"

—Kristin Muyskens, M.A., L.P.; psychologist

"Donna Chicone's *Being a Super Pet Parent* is a fun and informative read that will leave you reflecting on how you can be the best pet parent you can be! Whether you are a new or experienced pet parent, Donna shares many 'hot tips' on a variety of topics you can try with your dog immediately. Ike, Eliza, and Kirby (three Portuguese water dogs) love Donna's ideas too!"

—Christine Peper, PhD

$\cdots\cdots\cdots\cdots\cdots\cdots$ ⦅ $\cdots\cdots\cdots\cdots\cdots\cdots$

BEING A

Super

PET PARENT

$\cdots\cdots\cdots\cdots\cdots\cdots$ ⦅ $\cdots\cdots\cdots\cdots\cdots\cdots$

BEING A
Super
PET PARENT

Everything
You Need to Know
to Foster a Long,
Loving
Relationship with
Your Dog

by

DONNA CHICONE

DANCING PAWS PRESS

This publication is designed to provide accurate and authoritative information in regard to the subject matter covered. It is sold with the understanding that the publisher is not engaged in rendering legal or professional services.

Socialization Checklist used by permission of the ASPCA.
List of Foods Dogs Should Not Eat used by permission of The Humane Society of the United States.
References to the Responsible Breeder Criteria and Breeds Lists used by permission of the American Kennel Club.
whendogstalk.com used by permission of Sarah Hodgson.
truthaboutpetfood.com used by permission of Susan Thixton.
dogfoodadvisor.com used by permission of Dog Food Advisor.

Cover photos by Laurie Erickson, photographybylauriejerickson.zenfolio.com
Interior photos taken by the author unless otherwise noted.

Library of Congress Control Number: 2015916242
ISBN: 978-0-9968108-0-7

Published by
Dancing Paws Press

Book design by Stacey Aaronson

Printed in the United States of America

While the author has made every effort to provide accurate Internet addresses and other resources at the time of publication, neither the publisher nor the author assumes any responsibility for errors or changes that occur after publication. Further, the publisher does not have any control over and does not assume any responsibility for author or third-party websites or their content.

This book is dedicated to all dogs
who need a loving family and a home

JAZZ & JIVE

Author's Note

This is the book I wanted but couldn't find when I got my first dog. Now, after more than a few missteps, several lessons learned, and acquiring a lot of thoughtful knowledge and experience over the years, I've created this comprehensive guide to allow pet parents to have access to all they need to know in one book about nurturing a healthy and loving relationship with their dogs.

Whether you're considering getting a dog for yourself or your family, you have a new dog, or you've been a pet parent for many years already, this book is for you. Being aware of your beloved canine's needs and making informed and responsible decisions for their well-being will promote an increased quality of life for them, as well as a loving, lasting bond between you. It is therefore my wish that this book will help you to foster a lifetime of understanding, respect, and love for your four-legged treasure ... and that it will be returned to you many times over.

Table of Contents

My Journey as a Pet Parent

Dogs are not our whole life, but they make our lives whole.
— Roger A. Caras,
American wildlife preservationist, photographer, and writer

I had just left a career in corporate America where I spent twenty-three years doing presentations and training in my various job responsibilities, and my plan was to create my own business as a professional speaker and trainer. In the beginning, I would be working almost exclusively from my home to establish the business, allowing me the time to bring a new dog into my life. It had been several years since I had a trusted companion by my side, and I was ready for more life in my home once again.

When I was working full-time in my corporate career, I had often thought about having a dog but knew my time was too committed to my job. I was physically away from home working and traveling — not a good situation for either a new dog or my family. Now, time — to a degree — was mine to manage, and I was excited about the prospects of both developing my business and nurturing a pet.

I knew that having a dog would mean focusing on caring for him or her, especially in the first few months. Yet, I believed I could still accomplish the work I needed to do for my business *and* add to our family, confident that the two would be in harmony. My husband was on board as well, so when the time would come for me to travel or be away for a speaking event, he would be able to care for the dog until I returned. With his support, I began my research.

This much planning for a dog may sound unnecessary to some people; however, I learned from my earlier experiences that adding a member to the family needs to be well thought out. Being a pet parent is a lifelong commitment, so it's only right that a lot of preparation go into the decision. Researching the individual needs of a particular breed, creating the right environment for the dog's development, and considering the timing of welcoming the new addition are vital to ensuring a match made in heaven, rather than a decade or more of frustration and inconvenience.

Back in 2006, I was three years out from grieving the loss of my first Portuguese water dog. I dearly loved Breezer, but unfortunately I made decisions about his welfare with limited information. Looking back now I can see how many things I could have done differently, contributing to a better quality of life for him. I was only walking and exercising him randomly at best; I was feeding him the same dry kibble every day with no variety or attention to what was in the ingredients. I did not continue training classes with him beyond puppy kindergarten and some basic obedience classes, nor did I develop his need to have a job, which would help work off his extraordinary energy. He was an intelligent and energetic dog who was loved, fed, and taken to the vet for basic care, but that was it. He could have had so much more quality experience in his lifetime, and I could have enjoyed my relationship with him much more and developed a bond where we both would have thrived. These were losses I wasn't even aware of at the time.

When I found Breezer, the breeder tried diligently to educate me about his breed, but the information fell on semi-deaf ears. I had my own ideas about how this venture was going to play out, and nothing else seemed able to influence me otherwise. I represented many first-time pet owners with a fantasy of how to bring a dog into my life – and how that experience would play out – which was a perspective truly not based on reality or much accurate information. I was honestly trying to be a good pet owner, but resources simply weren't as prevalent then as they are now, not to mention that the focus of training was not as positive in application as it is today.

Breezer
1991–2001

The theory of training a dog at that time was based on the need to be dominant – that the human needed to be "alpha" in the relationship. This approach did not promote a respectful partnership, but rather a power-status relationship between the human and the dog. Not having a sense of what was positive or negative in training and caring for a dog, I merely did the best I could with the limited knowledge I had. This meant I was frustrated much of the time and so was Breezer. We often had difficulty knowing what we needed and wanted from each other.

After the initial obedience classes when Breezer was a puppy, I did not incorporate training into our daily routines or provide him with opportunities to develop his skills. Working dogs, like Portuguese water dogs, need jobs and a purpose or their energy becomes directed toward negative behavior, such as chewing and destroying their human's belongings. This energy therefore commands guidance in positive directions – a form of training like obedience, agility, or even Animal Assisted Therapy work. But because I hadn't fully absorbed what the breeder told me, Breezer became a stay-at-home pet who was loved and received food and shelter – but he didn't receive the training and responsibilities he needed and deserved. As a result, Breezer truly gave more to us than I believe we were able to give back to him. Of course, like all dogs, he did so without complaining. In fact, he demonstrated enthusiasm and great love for us at all times, no matter what, until his last days on earth.

During Breezer's lifetime, I met a wonderful groomer who told me about a breeder of Portuguese water dogs she highly respected. When I was ready for another dog, I made the decision to contact her and from that moment, a great friendship and working relationship developed between us. Soon, a brown and wavy-coated Portuguese water dog I named Jazz came into my life, bringing with him the joy and exuberance he naturally shares.

I went to see Jazz as a puppy in his litter three times before we actually brought him home. I was also able to meet Java, his wonderful doggie mother. The puppies in the litter thrived with the tender loving care of Java and the breeders, Katie and Cindy, who did an excellent job developing the puppies. They socialized them to new sounds and experiences, children and adults, trips to the veterinary clinic, new textures and tastes – everything developing puppies need to be exposed to. I told Katie I specifically wanted a dog who could do Animal Assisted Therapy as an adult, so temperament figured greatly in my selection process. I worked professionally as a therapist and knew a dog would have a positive impact on people in this environment. I was actually quite clear about this goal for myself and my soon-to-be dog.

We brought Jazz home to join our family when he was nine weeks old, and my life changed forever.

My experience in finding Katie and her helping me find Jazz was the beginning of my introduction to what I considered a "movement" in the dog world. Every person I met − whether a trainer, breeder, veterinarian, or even many pet owners − appeared to be an advocate for dogs. All of them wanted to make the world a better place for dogs and the humans who loved them. And I wanted to be part of this movement.

As this was important to me and something I believed in, I desired to do what I could to help make a difference. My skills were primarily in the media, where I learned to produce TV shows in my corporate career. Things miraculously came together and soon I had my own show, *The Dog Show with Jazz*, on community access television. This happened so naturally that it soon became my full-time job. My intention to build a speaking and training business went to the back burner, and the show became my professional focus.

With Jazz by my side as my featured co-host, my guests included breeders, trainers, and other experts in the dog world who shared their knowledge with our viewers. The show received a regional Emmy nomination, which was a gratifying affirmation of the quality of the show, confirming that it brought a message and information about dogs people wanted to hear.

I produced and hosted forty-eight shows, gaining a wealth of knowledge from the research I did prior to each show, as well as from the many professionals I encountered in the world of dogs. I also spent hours exploring the best nutrition, health supplements, training programs, trainers, and general care for my dogs. It was a never-ending journey learning new things to ensure a quality life for my dog − and I loved it!

Four years after Jazz became a member of our family (and still doing our TV show), I decided it was time to bring another dog into our lives. I'd never had two dogs before and wasn't sure how to prepare for this life-changing experience, so I once again contacted Katie, our friend and breeder, and told her of my desire to find another Portuguese water dog. I wanted this second dog to be suited for Animal Assisted Therapy work as well, and knowing Jazz, Katie felt he would do better with a female versus a male dog in his life.

Similar to finding Jazz, I visited the litter and met mama Breezy, who was a doting and loving mother, and Jive, a brown female − the smallest in the litter. She was bottle-fed until she was able to nurse on her own, and I was able to feed her during my visits, initiating the bond between us.

When we picked Jive up and transitioned her from her litter to our family, we brought Jazz with us to meet her. They were instant friends and bonded more every day they spent together.

I also incorporated Jive into segments of the TV show, making us a team of three.

I went from focusing on one dog to two; everything was double – the devotion of time as well as the cost of food, toys, crates, vet care, and training. But most of all, I had twice the love.

We often hear people say they learn a lot from their dogs, and I have found this to be true in my experience with Jazz and Jive. The time spent with them has been a most insightful and even spiritual experience, changing me from a naïve, undereducated dog owner to a committed, responsible human parent to my beloved dogs and an advocate for all canines.

While I am not a trainer, I have spent hundreds of hours training my own dogs. With former careers as a nurse and as a family and addictions counselor, I have found that experience to influence my thinking and behavior with my dogs, specifically influencing my relationship with them and how that bond develops and grows over time.

During my time as a counselor, I met with numerous families and individuals, helping them see how their behavior was impacting themselves and the people around them – including their pets. Just as humans feel deeply, it is important to integrate a dog into a family or individual relationship by honoring the dog as a sensitive and social being within that relationship. This is done best when all family members can express and trust their feelings and are able to respect the sensitive nature of the dog as well.

I especially remember a director of one of the treatment programs where I worked as an addictions counselor. Whenever he did an intake evaluation for someone coming into the program, one of the questions he asked was, "Did you ever hit or hurt your dog when you were high or using your mood-altering chemical?" Research today shows what we knew then: that where there is abuse of drugs and alcohol and physical abuse of human family members, there is also often abuse of the family pet.

This is a vivid example of how dogs are impacted by the behavior of family members. The central focus of treatment in an addiction program is the individual taking responsibility for their behavior. This of course transfers to all people in every type of living situation – we are all responsible for our behavior and for our relationship commitments, and a relationship with a dog demands that same commitment. Dogs are not disposable items. They are living, breathing members of families and society. Being attentive to our dogs and their feelings is essential; this insight has guided me in my relationships with my dogs to be responsible and accountable in my behavior toward them until the time our relationship will end.

For Jazz and Jive's training, for example, I implement only positive methods. That means no verbal or physical abuse or use of harmful training tools like prong collars, shock collars, or any tool or practice that will cause the dog to feel pain or stress. Spending time with my dogs is a priority for me. I also talk to my dogs all the time. All of these practices promote harmony in our family.

Part of my advocacy for dogs is to help all of us as humans become more sensitive to the reality that our dogs are sentient beings who experience pain, fear, and joy. In the world of grammar etiquette, it is correct to reference animals as "that" and "it," but you may have already noticed that I don't follow that convention. I want to encourage us to refer to dogs as "who" and "him" or "her." Why? Because referring to our beloved dogs as the feeling beings they are is the beginning of making a difference in our relationship together. As such, you will find my references to our dogs in the "being" reference, which is viewed technically as *grammatically* incorrect, but in my view as *humanely* correct.

I know there are many pet parents who want to do the best they can to provide a good life for their dogs. If you are someone who is less informed about caring properly for the wonderful dogs you love like I once was, having thoughtful information will allow you to make better decisions for them.

Again, I didn't realize how uninformed I was with Breezer until I brought Jazz and Jive into my life and had an entirely different learning experience as a pet parent. That happened in part because I was more receptive as a person, and in part because there was new and helpful information available that was easily accessible. This is my wish for all people who have a dog in their lives – that they may be informed pet parents. Education and understanding goes a long way. I hope you continue reading.

Woofs & Smiles!

Donna Chicone

PART ONE

So You Want to Become a Pet Parent

Wʜᴀᴛ Mᴏᴛɪᴠᴀᴛᴇꜱ Uꜱ ᴛᴏ Wᴀɴᴛ ᴀ Dᴏɢ ɪɴ Oᴜʀ Lɪᴠᴇꜱ?

Happiness is a warm puppy.
— Cʜᴀʀʟᴇꜱ M. Sᴄʜᴜʟᴢ, *cartoonist*

There is nothing more adorable or capable of melting a heart than a puppy. Actually, a baby in almost any species is guaranteed to elicit "oohs" and "aahs" from most humans. Babies make us feel good and bring a smile to our faces. I have watched segments on TV where news anchors who are typically factual in presenting news information completely soften and become more relaxed when they do a spot on puppies – or babies of any species for that matter.

Disney movies about dogs also promote the cuteness factor and encourage us to think of dogs as "more like us." They talk and follow a story line we can relate to, usually with a favorable ending. I remember when I was a young child and saw *Lady and the Tramp*. I cried and rooted for Tramp to win over and save Lady. Of course he did and they lived happily ever after.

Even as an adult I am still intrigued with a good Disney film; in fact, I notice that most movies about animals seem to bring joy to our lives. The problem is, we can easily fall in love with the notion of having the ideal dog – just like in the movies – desiring to duplicate that wonderful feeling by bringing a dog from that specific breed into our family, often without much upfront preparation. As a result, there is genuine concern in the dog world when a movie about a breed of dog becomes popular with the general public, such as 101 *Dalmatians*, *Lassie*, *The Shaggy Dog*, and *Beethoven*, to name just a few of a long list. The fallout is often the proliferation of irresponsible breeders who propagate a specific dog for the sake of making money on the current popularity of that breed.

At times like this, breed-specific rescue groups must take on the task of rescuing as many of their breed as possible from the animal shelters — where the dogs are usually dropped off after the honeymoon of having the puppy, who has now grown into an adult dog, is over. Even a situation like President Obama selecting a Portuguese water dog to join his family caused many breeders and owners I know to become concerned for the potential welfare of our breed. The Portuguese water dog clubs and the responsible breeders I am in contact with all decided to use this as an opportunity to educate the public, and part of that education is that the Portuguese water dog is not a pet for everyone. Katie, my friend and breeder, often says, "There's a reason you don't see as many Portuguese water dogs on the street as you do golden retrievers." A golden retriever is easy to train and wants to please its human trainer, while a Portuguese water dog is intelligent and trainable, but will often challenge the human trainer with his independent behavior.

A woman once contacted me who had had dogs all her life but had been without one for some time. Having decided she wanted a dog again, a friend of ours suggested she might like having a Portuguese water dog. While this breed is not unlike having any other dog — which involves a sincere commitment of time and money, regular grooming, and daily exercise — Portuguese water dogs require more than the typical breed, not to mention they need a job, such as a canine sport like agility, or service work like Animal Assisted Therapy to perform on a regular basis. As such, the time and energy commitment is greater. If one hasn't had a dog before, this may not be the right breed; because of their intelligence and independent nature, they can also be challenging to train.

The woman came to my home and met Jazz and Jive in person. She was immediately drawn to the dogs, and it was lovely to see her comfort level around them. Because she traveled frequently, however, she had concerns for the dog's care in her absence, as any pet parent would. Though she had a friend who might care for him when she was away, she wasn't aware of the amount of work that went into grooming, or the maintenance between grooming appointments. For example, if this breed is not brushed fairly regularly, the coat will mat, causing discomfort. She also didn't have a fenced-in backyard for this high-energy dog to run and exercise.

Grateful for the opportunity to meet the dogs and for the honest discussion, she concluded that having a Portuguese water dog was not a good fit for her. Had she jumped into owning this breed without an understanding of its needs, as many people do with dogs of all breeds, she likely would have become frustrated and overwhelmed, ultimately giving the dog up for adoption, or denying the dog some of his fundamental needs.

The bottom line is: due diligence is required before adopting any animal – not just a dog. Any pet owner must have the full picture in mind of what it takes to have a particular animal or breed, ensuring they have the resources, time, and devotion to care for that pet for the duration of his or her life. Pets are reliant on us as children are, and we must see that reliance as a responsibility we don't take lightly.

People have various motives for bringing a dog into their lives. Some are driven by emotion or impulsive decision; others by practical need or thoughtful consideration of their family or other pets. Some of the motives I've heard are:

- I have always wanted a (specific breed name).

- I always knew I wanted to rescue a dog from a shelter.

- I grew up with dogs in my family and want to have a dog in my own family now.

- The kids need a playmate; a dog would be perfect.

- My dog needs another dog to play with.

- My neighbor's dog is so cute; I want a dog just like theirs.

- I want a small white dog who doesn't shed to go with the décor of my home.

- I want a dog to hunt with.

- I want a dog to carry around like a baby and dress up in cute clothes.

- I want a dog who is suited to do Animal Assisted Therapy work.

- I want a service dog to help me improve my quality of life.

- I want a watchdog for my home.

- I want the company of a dog in my life.

- I want a smaller dog to travel with me.

- I want a fierce dog others fear so people won't mess with me.

Though there are many more reasons than these, the truth is that we may simply want a dog to experience being loved. Paul J. Zak, professor of economics at Claremont Graduate University and the author of *The Moral Molecule: The Source of Love and Prosperity*, said: "Neurochemical research has shown that the hormone released when people are in love is released in animals in the same intimate circumstances. We also found that dogs reduced stress hormones better than cats."

Zak's extensive research also indicates that dogs may feel love for each other and for others, including humans (I don't think we have to convince most pet parents of this, but research is always nice to have as confirmation!). If being with a dog can feel so good, it's no wonder so many of us want to have a dog in our lives. What's important is to be as clear as possible with our motive. This allows us to make the best decision about when and what kind of dog to bring into our home – or if we should pursue acquiring a dog at all.

·············· The Perils of Gift Giving ··············

Our love affair with puppies often causes many to believe they'd make adorable Christmas and birthday gifts. But while gifting a puppy is a lovely intention, it is actually inappropriate for both the puppy and the human receiving her.

For one, when dogs are connected to celebrations like birthdays and holidays, it is frequently a decision based more on emotion than logic. At a holiday or other festive time, a dependent and helpless puppy will surely not receive the attention he or she requires, which is essential to starting off well in a new home. The focus is spread to so many other activities that the puppy's needs get lost in the shuffle.

Two, giving a puppy as a gift can also create bonding issues with the human recipient and the puppy. Bonding begins the moment you see the dog you know is for you – that is the beginning of the commitment in the relationship. As such, the person responsible for the dog's care ideally needs to have a say about which dog that will be.

In my early adult years, I received a puppy as a gift from a boyfriend. I knew his intention was good, and while I thought the puppy was cute, my boyfriend was the one who chose her – and he was the one who was initially smitten by her. I did not really want a puppy, but I didn't want to hurt his feelings and decided to find a way to make it work.

The truth is, I had no business keeping this dog. I was working full-time as a nurse and living in a house with six other nurses who all worked different shifts. People were coming in and out of the house at all hours, confusing this helpless puppy about which human she could depend on. I was focused on my job and my social life, and while I thought the puppy was adorable and wanted to take care of her, I didn't know the first thing about what I needed to do for her – and worse, I did not make a huge effort to learn. At a certain point, I left nursing to fly with a national airline as a flight attendant, and my then puppy "Tish" was generously and lovingly adopted by Sandy, one of my nursing roommates. Tish lived her life to the ripe old age of thirteen with Sandy and her husband David. I was then – and am still now – ever so grateful to them for taking her into their lives at a time when I couldn't be the devoted pet parent my little girl deserved.

While this experience took place many years ago when my notion of having a dog was markedly different than it is today, the bottom line was that I was an irresponsible pet parent to Tish. Even though I loved her dearly, she needed much more than what I was able to give her. She was a sweet gift, but as I said, an inappropriate one. The person responsible for the dog is the one who must make the decision to adopt and to commit to being a pet parent, *not* be surprised with the sudden appearance of a dog as a "gift." To the well intentioned and romantics out there: jewelry and flowers make much better surprise presents.

The desire to have a dog is also often seen in people who want to foster responsibility or have company for their children. In this situation, much thought needs to be given to what kind of dog would be best for your family. Do you purchase from a reputable breeder or adopt? Do you want an older dog or younger dog? Most importantly, who will have primary responsibility for the dog? A young child, for example, should never be made completely responsible for a pet; the adult must be the model and demonstrate being a responsible human parent to a dog.

Being involved in caring for a dog also needs to be aligned properly with the age of the child. A ten-year-old clearly can assume more responsibility than a three-year-old. For instance, an older child can be entrusted to play games like fetch with the dog in the backyard, reinforcing and practicing previously trained behaviors like sit, come, stay, and leave it. A toddler, on the other hand, needs active supervision at all times. Not only does he need to be taught how to pet a dog without hurting or alarming her, he needs to be taught not to jump on the dog, or to ride a big dog like a horse. Safety for the dog and the child is the number one concern.

In short, engaging the child in a positive learning experience will promote the bond between the child and the dog, which could certainly last a lifetime, but dogs and young children need to be supervised at all times for the safety of both.

Finally, it is important to think about what happens if things don't work out. Many think it's okay to surrender the dog to an animal shelter because it did not meet the intended purpose, which was to make the children happy. I know people who have described this very scenario to me, relating that the pet was a good dog but did not get the training he needed to transition well into the family. Because families can rightly feel overwhelmed with their numerous obligations on top of caring for and training a dog, it is not a decision to take lightly, not to mention that it is unfair to the dog. Another scenario I hear is that the dog truly did not match up well with the children – he simply needed to be in a family without children or with only one child.

If any of these are the case and the family/dog relationship doesn't work out, taking responsibility to find a good home for a dog you can no longer keep is a much better option than surrendering him to a shelter, where there is a high probability that he will be euthanized.

In sum, I know many people who have brought a dog into their family primarily for their child or children, and it has worked out to everyone's benefit. Growing up with a dog can be one of the most memorable and loving experiences for both a dog and a child – but parents must do their homework first. Although it's impossible to guarantee a favorable relationship with a pet over time, if the dog and family are well matched from the start and everyone's responsibilities for the particular breed are clear, they can both likely look forward to many wonderful years of bonding and love.

· · · · · · · · · · · · · · The Desire to Rescue · · · · · · · · · · · · · ·

Another significant motivation influencing people to bring a dog into their lives is that they genuinely want to rescue dogs from their plight in shelters and give them a better life. The Humane Society of the United States estimates that animal shelters care for six to eight million dogs and cats every year in the United States, of whom approximately three to four million are euthanized.

Humane animal shelters feel the impact of overpopulation more than anyone else. These shelters require financial support to house dogs and cats without the need to euthanize – which in most cases happens after only three days or less. A hopeful goal is for all shelters to be no-kill, but this means having more money and staff, not to mention volunteers to walk dogs and help with other aspects of care.

. . . .

If you're a dog lover and have a dog, or if you can't or don't have one, volunteering at a shelter is a great way to give back and become educated about dogs at the same time.

. . . .

While shelters strive to do as much as they can and always want to do more, they are challenged by a lack of funds, with more animals than they can care for. The "disposable dog syndrome" in our country has created a climate of disrespect and disregard for dogs; viewing a dog as something that can be surrendered at any time or because things don't seem to be working out only contributes to the overpopulation problem. This almost always occurs simply because a dog has not been trained. For this reason, shelters aim daily to help people become responsible pet parents who are educated and able to provide loving homes and a good life for their dog.

A hands-on method shelters use to achieve this goal is to offer classes and training programs for new pet parents in all kinds of situations. Someone may need guidance on caring for a dog with an abusive background or special needs, or for preparing a dog for a new family member or baby arriving. Or they may simply need basic training to influence their dog's good behavior. I know a lot of people who have successfully adopted a dog from a shelter, but they have spent time training and working with them. While it may be easy to believe that merely bringing a dog into your home is enough to make him happy and adjusted, that's simply not the case. A home is certainly more than the dog would have had if he stayed in the shelter or was euthanized, but training enhances a dog's life in immeasurable ways.

On a walk one day with both my dogs, I met a woman with her rescue dog who appeared to be a Border Collie/Labrador mix. She was delightful and had only recently adopted him. The dog was jumping all over the place and seemed to want to play with my dogs — or anything that would play with him. He was about two years old and quite puppy-like with his behavior. When I asked if he could say "hello" to my dogs, she said, "Yes, but he jumps all the time. I don't know what to do to make him stop." My dogs remained calm as hers continued to jump. I then asked if I could give her dog a treat. She agreed, and within seconds he was sitting calmly and took the treat with a gentle mouth. I could tell he was a good dog who simply needed training. He clearly had her love, but he needed more.

While we will talk in length about training in Chapters Nine and Ten, I can't emphasize enough that we *must* realize the importance of training for our dogs. It is our responsibility to train them in the same way we guide our children so that they know how to live in our world. We cannot expect them to know the rules on their own; we need to teach them. In fact, training is a dog's right. When we facilitate positive training, it is always a win-win for the dog and the human.

Being clear about why we want a dog in our lives is the first vital step when considering a special canine companion — not only for us, but for the dog as well. Next, we must be cognizant of the dog's particular needs; without proper research and realistic expectations, we may set ourselves up for a negative outcome. There is a plethora of great books on training, nutrition, and more for dogs; you can also Google any topic about dogs and return a huge selection of articles and websites. In addition, I have listed several books and trainers' websites with excellent reputations that you may find helpful in the Resources section of this book.

Interacting with people who are committed to helping dogs is an education of its own. Every day there is more research helping us understand dogs, how they relate to us, and why. You can find clubs for specific breeds and rescue groups for almost every purebred, as well as for all mixed breeds, who will be happy to answer your questions. And as we ultimately want to see fewer dogs in shelters, remember that adoption opportunities abound in shelters across the country.

Acquiring sound information beforehand will not only help you make the best decision about which type of dog to bring into your life, but it will also help you to enjoy the optimum outcome when you make that lifelong commitment.

Trust your own intuition and intelligence. Both will serve you well.

CHAPTER TWO

RESPECTING OUR DIFFERENCES
AND RESPONDING APPROPRIATELY

If you pick up a starving dog and make him prosperous, he will not bite you; that is the principal difference between a dog and a man.

— MARK TWAIN

In successful situations, dogs and humans thrive together from a mutual respect of each other and of the differences between us. For example, we look and smell different to them; we don't speak "dog," and dogs don't speak human. Dogs accept these differences and respect us for being the humans we are, relating to us in ways other animals do not. They even seem to understand that we need them, particularly if we are hurting or going through a tough time. If a human bonds with a dog, the love between them can be very powerful. Anyone who has experienced that type of relationship will tell you how constant a dog's love can be.

The physical differences between us are obvious: Dogs walk on four legs and have jaws that can rip toys and most anything they can get a good grip on. They are trained to poop and pee outdoors (in most cases), and they have an incredible sense of smell. The ability to track a scent is one of their strongest, if not *the* strongest, ability, making them able to sniff out substances from drugs to cancer, locate lost persons, and much more. We are only beginning to appreciate all they can do with their scent abilities.

Despite these obvious differences between a dog and a human being, however, people sometimes liken their dog to a child and treat him as they would a human child. Yes, we think like humans, but when we relate to our dogs as humans, the line can become blurred when we assign childlike expectations to them, presuming they'll behave accordingly. Then, when dogs behave like dogs, we often react with confusion and disappointment – and may even blame the dog for not behaving as we expected.

My veterinarian friends have shared numerous stories of having to remind the client that a dog is different from a child or person. Many of us know someone who has a dog, often a small breed, who they dress up and talk to like a baby. This dog usually has not been trained and is treated like a child. Take my friend, for example, who has a four-pound Yorkie. She takes her dog everywhere in her purse, which I personally find a wonderful benefit to having a small dog. (I could never have a purse big enough for Jazz or Jive!) She loves buying clothes for her, and she communicates with her using baby talk. My friend enjoys this very much and I believe she thinks her dog enjoys it too, but whenever I see the dog, I can tell she wants to play and go outdoors. She also jumps a lot, which is tolerated due to her small size.

Because small dogs are so physically manageable, the idea of training them is often lost. Picking them up and showering them with affection seems like enough. Yet, the dogs I know in these situations are yearning to be outside playing in the dirt, running around sniffing whatever they can find of interest to their dog nature and instincts. Left unfulfilled, this instinct can shift toward being reactive – both to dogs and humans – because the dog was not socialized to other dogs, people, or even play. Any dog, regardless of size, who is reactive toward humans or other dogs is not fun to be with for any length of time.

To further explain these differences, take my dog, Jive. She definitely looks like a female and is attractive – she's actually considered pretty for a dog. Looking at her all groomed and sitting quietly, she conjures up feelings of sweetness that make you want to hold her or hug her – or at the very least pet her a lot, which she will let almost anyone do endlessly (she quite respectfully finds her way into the personal space of each person she meets so they can do so).

But despite her girlie exterior, Jive is still a dog. She digs holes in my backyard that cover her face and paws with dirt, which quickly becomes backwash in the water bowl and tracked into my house. She chases Jazz, who is twenty pounds heavier than she is, and nips at his private parts to get him to give up the toy he is keeping from her. What's more, she eats poop (rabbit raisins, Jazz's, and who knows what else). She hates wearing anything like a bow in her hair and shakes it off within seconds. Jazz has never destroyed a stuffed toy in his lifetime, yet Jive destroys every single toy she gets a hold of. These are not qualities that can be likened to a little human girl who likes to cuddle with stuffed animals and hold tea parties. Jive behaves like a dog. Expecting her to behave like a sweet little girl is totally unrealistic.

The tendency for us to treat dogs like children could be that some developmental behaviors are similar. Puppies, like children, do not come into the world with instructions. We do our best to meet their needs when they don't have words to tell us what it is they need at the moment. While children eventually use words, however, we never have that advantage with dogs. But what remains the same between them is that puppies and children both need love and nurturing. Dogs require training to live in our human-controlled society, just as children must learn acceptable behavior and good manners. And that responsibility, whether to dogs or children, falls to the humans they live with. As human parents to our canine family members, problems arise when we forget our differences, despite their ability to connect to and understand us.

Researcher Stanley Coren, PhD, of the University of British Columbia has determined that dogs' mental abilities are close to a human child aged two to two and a half. Coren says:

> The intelligence of various types of dogs does differ and the dog's breed determines some of these differences. There are three types of dog intelligence: instinctive (what the dog is bred to do), adaptive (how well the dog learns from their environment to solve problems), and working and obedience (the equivalent of 'school learning').

The "instinctive" learning Dr. Coren refers to makes good sense – each breed of dog is bred for a purpose. For example, the Portuguese water dog went to sea with the Portuguese fishermen and worked the nets in the sea. They actually dove deep into the waters and herded fish to the nets, working hard all day and taking messages from boat to boat and boat to shore by swimming in the open waters. They had to make decisions on their own (to know when sharks were in the water), and they developed a sound work ethic and incredible stamina. This breed continues to have great physical stamina, and they are quite intelligent. If you don't keep them busy and challenged, they will find ways to meet those needs – which is usually creative on their part and upsetting to the humans around them.

As I mentioned in Chapter One, because of the energy they carry that's meant for a job, this breed needs a pet parent who will be able to positively direct this energy. With Jazz and Jive, for example, I involve them in the sport of K9 Nose Work and Animal Assisted Therapy. I also have built-in jobs for them around the house, like retrieving the toy they've taken outside, which is nearly every time they go into the yard.

But Portuguese water dogs are not the only ones with employable skills. When I did my TV show, I invited many different breeders on the show to tell our audience about their breed, and I asked them to be clear about the history of the breed, as that always translates into present-day dog behavior. This is true for all breeds.

The American Kennel Club identifies breed classifications based on the purposes for which dogs were bred. For example, the Working Group, which includes the Portuguese water dog, boxer, Newfoundland, St. Bernard, and rottweiler, to name only a few, are all bred with a similar focus on working.

The Australian shepherd is a breed in the Herding Group. This breed was bred to herd sheep and worked hard by the farmer's side all day. I have had owners tell me their Aussie (Australian shepherd) will herd the children, and one owner told me her Aussie would even try to herd the cars parked on the street! This is the perfect example of how instinctive behavior cannot be bred out of dogs. To engage that instinct in this breed, Aussies love sports that require agility, actual herding training classes, or learning to catch Frisbees – and of course dog tricks are always fun for the dog and the trainer.

Another group, the Sporting Group, identifies those bred to hunt. The golden retriever and Labrador are two of the most popular breeds in the United States; with instinctive hunting behavior and a desire to please their human, they can be fun to train. To keep a sporting group dog busy, canine sports like agility or K9 Nose Work, or anything requiring hunting skills, are great choices. They also love to retrieve and can be taught to catch and return balls, Frisbees, or similar safe objects. Again, tricks are engaging and fun for all dogs and trainers.

· · · · · · · · · · · · ·

The American Kennel Club (AKC) identifies seven breed groups: Herding, Hound, Non-Sporting, Terrier, Toy, Working, Foundation Stock Services, and a Miscellaneous Class. There are over 460 breeds of dogs in the world. The AKC recognizes 164 breeds today.

· · · · · · · · · · · · ·

If you have a rescue dog who is comprised of more than one breed, it is crucial to note that all of those breeds can influence your dog's behavior in some way. For this reason, it is beneficial to learn about each breed represented in your dog to help you better understand him. You can purchase canine DNA kits online and in reputable pet stores to find out which breeds make up your dog. The cost ranges from $70 to $100 and requires only a simple swabbing of the dog's mouth to submit for testing.

No matter what the breed of your pet, the more you know about your dog's breed will help you understand your dog's behavior, which ultimately leads to a happy family.

·············· Developing a Relationship ············· with Our Dogs

There has been much written and taught over the past years about needing to be in an alpha relationship with your dog — meaning that you need to be dominant over him. The alpha concept is believed to be an aspect of wolves' behavior in packs, and since dogs are descendants of the wolf, it made sense to many trainers and other dog experts to mimic this dynamic with dogs. I personally always struggled with the whole alpha concept, precisely because it commanded that I exert some physical sense of dominance over my dogs, and I was never completely comfortable in that role.

I remember a trainer once suggested I put Jazz in a submissive position by turning him on his back and holding him down, which elicited a perplexed look from Jazz. I felt rather embarrassed and never did it again; instinctively, I knew it was unnecessary. Jazz and I had a positive and respectful relationship then as we do now. Such an act of dominance would have only served to harm our connection, and it would have had no favorable outcome that I could see.

Thankfully, more is now being written and taught about disregarding the alpha approach and focusing on relationships with our dogs based on building a positive bond. Just as in raising a child, respect and positive communication are much more effective than dominance and negative reinforcement.

In her book, *Animals Make Us Human*, Temple Grandin cites the research of Dr. L. David Mech, who conducted a thirteen-year study of the wolves on Ellesmere Island in the Northwest Territories of Canada. Dr. Mech's findings were vital as they changed what we thought was true about wolves for centuries:

> In the wild, wolves don't live in wolf packs, and they don't have an alpha male who fights the other wolves to maintain his dominance.

Temple Grandin goes on to explain:

> Our whole image of wolf packs and alphas is completely wrong. Instead, wolves live like people do: in a family made up of a mom, a dad, and the children.

These findings impact dogs because of their link to the wolf, leading Grandin to suggest that:

> ... dogs need parents, not pack leaders; what dogs probably need isn't a substitute pack leader but a substitute parent. I say that because genetically dogs are juvenile wolves, and young wolves live with their parents and siblings.

Temple Grandin's work and Dr. Mech's research support the premise that we should be a human parent to a canine member of our family – we are "parents" in the family system, not "alpha" members, and we are responsible for maintaining the welfare of all family members and respecting the differences in species.

Even without an alpha leader, however, dogs do have a social hierarchy and status, whereby dogs with higher social status can direct the "lower status" dogs. This instinctual understanding among dogs provides order in the family systems – and this carries over with dogs residing in human families. Canines feel respect and some degree of knowledge of the differences between themselves and their human parents, and people must reflect that to their pets. This is the best strategy for a functional and har-monious home — one that fosters respect and love for everyone. The bottom line is: domination doesn't work well with humans, so why would we expect it to enhance our relationships with our canine friends?

A trainer I admire, Sarah Hodgson, has a wonderful slogan that defines her work: "Don't Dominate — Communicate." Sarah is a positive and creative trainer who is a great resource for new or experienced pet parents. Not only is her website full of information, but she also writes articles on dog training for *The Huffington Post*. I genuinely respect her methods and en-courage people to visit her at whendogstalk.com.

As Sarah promotes, my relationship with both Jazz and Jive is built on respecting our differences. It is also built on fostering communication through positive means. It may sound funny, but I am always trying to think like a dog (as I anticipate they might understand or need something from a dog's point of view), and they are both constantly reading my body language and responding to the tone of my voice. In a mutual exchange, we are consis-tently striving to figure out what the other wants or needs. During this process, we have come to know each other quite well over the years.

Recently, I somehow developed muscle soreness in my lower back to the point that when a spasm occurred, I would instantly yell out in pain. One morning, I was brushing my hair in the bathroom and experienced a spasm. I immediately yelled out. Jazz was outside in the backyard, and when he heard me, he sat looking up at the bathroom window, barking. I was touched by his concern. But true to his nature, as I was watching him, I saw his eye catch a squirrel. ZOOM like a bullet he was gone. Jazz loves me very much, but he is a dog after all, and this particular squirrel had been eluding him for years.

During our many hours of training and living together, I have learned a lot about Jazz and Jive that has helped me to inform pet parents of all breeds. When Jive arrived, for instance, I became more tuned in to Jazz because I could see how different they were from each other; even when they're the same breed, all dogs have their own distinct personality. For example, Jazz is happy to be the center of attention while Jive is much more reserved.

Jazz is high energy and Jive is a cuddler. Jazz is a comedian and makes me laugh with his antics, and Jive is intelligent but asserts herself in a more reserved and quiet way than Jazz. Acknowledging those differences is essential to establishing a mutually respectful, loving relationship with each dog.

I remember before my son came into my life I would see a group of three-year-old children and generalize their behavior as being similar. While this may be true overall, if I were to talk with the childcare provider for that group of children, he/she would be able to tell me distinct differences about each child. If I were to then speak with the parent of one of the children, I would likely hear a lengthy discussion of all the attributes and behaviors of their child. How does the parent know their child so well? From spending time with them – playing, teaching, setting boundaries, and simply enjoying being together. The same process allows us to get to know our dogs, only between two different species. Yes, we can generalize all dogs' behavior as being similar, but as we spend time playing, training, setting boundaries, and enjoying our dog, we learn their likes, dislikes, needs, and specific behaviors and what they mean. All relationships take time to grow.

When we bring a dog into our lives, it is our role and responsibility to guide them with love. And while I am encouraging us to think of ourselves as pet parents, it's crucial that we remember our dogs are not human children. When we accept our dogs as the wonderful canines they are, a lifelong bond develops and the relationship can flourish with positive training and time together. Our dogs commit everything to us, and returning the favor is the least we can do to ensure a healthy relationship with our canine family members.

TIME, MONEY, AND RESPONSIBILITY

My goal is to be the person my dog thinks I am.
— AUTHOR UNKNOWN

The process of integrating a dog into a human family involves three major commitments: time, money, and responsibility – none of which can be taken lightly. The last thing you want is to feel guilty that you haven't the time to care for the living creature you brought into your family – one who waits patiently (or sometimes impatiently) for your return to the humble abode. The costs of pet ownership must also be budgeted into the family expenses. Aside from nutrition and yearly vet bills, there may be emergencies, additional training costs, and more. Then there's the responsibility to ensure that your pet is a respectable member of society. They must be integrated into your home and your neighborhood to ensure their safety as well as the safety of those around them.

· · · · · · · · · · · · The Commitment of Time · · · · · · · · · · ·

Dogs live for our companionship, yet our lives are filled with work, friends, neighbors, social engagements, you name it. Dogs, however, don't understand those outside commitments – they want to be with us as much as possible. In short, we are their entire world. They look to us for everything:

food, shelter, love, play, companionship, help when they are hurt or sick, or simply to be in their presence. Why do you think your dog is so eager to see you when you come home? It's merely a small demonstration of how much he loves and appreciates being with you.

In our family, when I come home, I make it a celebration. I kneel down to my dogs' level to pet them and tell them how happy I am to see them, specifically petting both dogs. This greeting lasts for a couple minutes, and then they go outside, which is the next phase of our coming-home routine. That time I give my dogs costs me nothing, but to them it is priceless.

In general, dogs are smart and easily adapt to our lifestyle and routines; they internalize our schedules, expect us to come and go at certain times of the day, and are aware of what we typically do when we're at home. When I take my walking shoes off the rack, for example, my dogs become excited. They both grab a soft toy in their mouths and begin trotting around, knowing they will be going for a walk soon. When I put on their scarf for therapy work, they demonstrate an eagerness and tail wag. Every pet parent I know experiences the same kind of behavior with his or her dog — their desire for quality time with us shows in a myriad of ways.

While having a grown dog with an established routine is great, many times we're starting out with a puppy, and just like an infant child, your puppy needs a lot of designated time with you to meet his needs. I have raised a human child from birth and two dogs each from nine weeks old, and for me personally, the puppies were more challenging in those early months. Contrary to what you may think, puppies demand a lot of attention, so it's vital to be prepared for this when you see that cute puppy and decide to bring him home.

The biggest commitment in these early days and weeks is related to potty training – or becoming house-trained – which requires a great deal of patience and time on the part of the human parent. Puppies under twelve weeks usually have no bladder or bowel control, so you will need to plan for someone to take him out every few hours. While each puppy is different, most can hold their bladder and bowels for time allotments equivalent to their age in months. For example, a three-month-old puppy could go three hours before needing to go outside.

Puppies also require touch and play time – your engagement with them is crucial as you teach them to respond to their name and learn the routine of the household. And like babies in the oral stage, they need to be surrounded with toys they can chew on so they don't destroy your personal articles. They must likewise be taught bite inhibition as you socialize them to humans and to dogs. A great way for them to enhance these skills is by attending "puppy kindergarten" classes, which begin at about sixteen weeks of age. (We will talk about this in detail in Chapter Ten.)

When you intentionally connect with your dog, all kinds of good things will happen for you – merely being with or petting a dog reduces blood pressure and heart rate, and it promotes a relaxed state. I've experienced this firsthand numerous times, as Jazz and Jive are trained therapy dogs. Whether working with children or adults, it is amazing to see – almost always – an automatic connection between the dog and the human, not to mention a faster change in desired behavior for the client than would occur without the dog's involvement. In fact, the physical, emotional, mental, and behavioral benefits to us as humans in relationships with dogs are becoming more and more documented in research today. Even Arianna Huffington in her book *Thrive* states that time spent with our animals is a way "to open our hearts and enhance our lives."

When I intentionally acknowledge my dogs' presence, everything seems better. Even simply cuddling or petting our dogs as we watch TV creates connection and greater relaxation, both for us and for our dogs. Positive – and I emphasize *positive* – quality time and touch is critical for our four-legged friends; your relationship must be built on loving experiences with them. For example, in providing the three "P"s – praise, patience, and petting

– we go a long way in nurturing trust and favorable behavior. We can be firm when needed, such as giving commands to keep them from harm's way, but there is never call to hit a dog with your hand or any article. Punishment is not what a dog needs, nor is yelling or screaming obscenities at them. Negative reinforcement doesn't work for humans, and it doesn't work for animals either.

As you spend time with your dog on a daily basis, he comes to know you are the one who feeds him, keeps him safe, plays with him, and takes him to the veterinarian for health reasons ... that you are in charge of meeting his basic and all other needs ... that you are the human parent setting the boundaries and providing what's wonderful in his life. Your thoughtful, caring interaction and reinforcement will strengthen the respect your dog has for you, alleviating the need for dominant behavior. Every bit of positive time you spend together goes a long way.

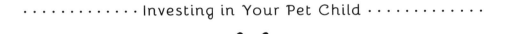

· · · · · · · · · · · · · Investing in Your Pet Child · · · · · · · · · · · ·

A 2012 USA *Today* article titled "Puppy Love" reported that as a country we spent $53 billion on pets in that one year alone, and according to the 2013–2014 National Pet Owners Survey by the American Pet Products Association, it costs over $1,000 a year to raise and nurture a dog. While the costs vary by age, breed, size, and health of the dog, as well as geography and climate – which affect flea and tick product costs – people seem to be committed to spending money for their dogs' needs despite a difficult economy. A friend once said to me, "We decide where we want to spend our money. I spend mine on my house. You put your money into your dogs." We all have our priorities, after all.

When we bring a dog into our lives, we need to accept up front that it will be for only a short time; the average length of a dog's life is ten to twelve years (with smaller breeds living longer than larger ones). Because our relative time with them is so limited, we should want it to be healthy and robust. As such, we must be committed to do whatever we can to accomplish that goal. The bottom line is, cost is a reality when you're a responsible human parent to your dog.

As I stated in Chapter One, getting a dog is often impulsive and emotionally driven, so it makes sense that fact-finding and research may not be a component of the upfront preparation. As a result, considering costs may not be a priority, and even when it is, most people greatly underestimate what those costs will be, especially if this is someone's first dog. Even published projected costs for dogs tend to underestimate the actual expenses. Although it's difficult to pinpoint, however, a general estimation still gives you a good guideline.

After conducting a great deal of research to determine the best food, grooming products, training, and health maintenance practices I can do myself, I have listed the following costs I've found quite close to a realistic annual expenditure for owning a dog the first year (many of which are ongoing yearly costs). Depending on the breed or breeds of your dog and size, activity level, etc., you may see costs fluctuate. Obviously, a larger breed eats more and in general needs everything larger, which usually costs more. And of course if you have more than one dog as I do, the number of dogs multiplies the costs.

Below is a breakdown of some initial and ongoing costs of owning a dog.

EXPENSE	INVESTMENT
Food and Treats	$250 – $1,000
Crates/Beds	$50 – $200
Leashes, Collars	$20 – $60
Toys	$25 – $150
Microchip, City License	$50 – $100
Grooming	$50 – $1,000
Routine Veterinary Care	$100 – $500
Preventive Medications, Vitamins & Supplements	$100 – $300
Training Classes	$60 – $300
Pet Sitters or Boarding	$100 – $300
Sports or Competition Events (optional)	$100 – $1,000*
Total Yearly Cost	**$905 – $4,910**
Monthly Cost	**$109 – $450**

The yearly total can be a shock to many people, seeming like a lot of money all at once – and this chart does not include any emergency situations. As such, it is important to consider the financial responsibility when thinking about bringing a dog into your life.

During the housing foreclosure crisis, many people who had a perfectly sound financial situation when they brought their dog home were forced to leave the family dog behind, primarily because they could no longer afford to care for her or take her with them. While this is a heartbreaking circumstance they of course couldn't foresee, it is still prudent to be money-wise about bringing a dog into your life, even in the best of situations.

If your budget does not allow for the ongoing cost of a dog, you may need to put the idea of becoming a pet parent on hold until the initial and ongoing maintenance costs are affordable. Once you and your family fall in love with your dog, it is even more difficult to not be able to provide for her needs, and in the worst-case scenario, you may have to give her up. Shelters receive numerous dogs due to this exact situation, and it is most unfortunate for all involved. No one wants to see a dog who once knew a loving family find herself in a shelter with many other fearful and anxious dogs all looking for homes.

· · · · · · · · · · · · · · · Added Responsibility · · · · · · · · · · · · · · ·

Because dogs were domesticated to live as companions with humans, they are required to learn how to live in a world controlled by human beings. As such, it is our responsibility as human parents to our dogs to prepare them for this.

Routines and schedules provide a sense of stability and trust for dogs just as they do for children and even for us as adults. When dogs feel safe and secure, they experience less stress; participating in your family and household routines is a perfect opportunity for them to have a job and a purpose (more on this in Chapter Ten). This can be as simple as meeting the children at the bus stop after school or bringing the toy back inside that they've taken outside, or as important as guarding the backyard and home, especially if you have a watchdog by breed influence. When I am gone, for instance, Jive will watch out the front window of the house while Jazz protects the back. Both dogs take this job seriously.

If you observe your dog in your daily activities, I'm sure you will notice behaviors he demonstrates that are repetitive and have meaning to him. Shape that behavior into a job-like experience and reward it until it is learned. Continue to acknowledge this behavior in a positive way. A common example would be your dog greeting people when they come to your home. You can train a dog to sit quietly and not bark when you open the door. I've trained my dogs to grab a soft toy when the doorbell rings or someone knocks on the door. They know fetching the toy is the acceptable behavior, while the jumping is not, plus it's harder for dogs to jump if they have something in their mouths.

As dogs can learn many behaviors, teaching them activities like bringing you a ball or toy to play with, or picking up their toys and putting them in a box or basket can allow you to reinforce good behavior. Be creative and think outside the box as you observe your dog. Above all, have fun together.

Ensuring Your Dog's Safety

Whether on a leash or in the house, you should know where your dog is at all times. When my dogs are in the backyard, for example, I check on them periodically to make sure they're within view and all right. You don't want your dogs escaping, getting into trouble, injuring themselves, or being taken by someone.

Weather is another vital consideration. Because dogs don't sweat like humans do, they respond to heat by panting and sweating from their paw pads. In hot weather, dogs can quickly overheat or experience heat exhaustion, which can be fatal if not treated immediately.

When we had dogs on the set doing the TV show, we knew they were too hot from the lights when we saw their wet paw prints on the studio floor. When this would happen, we removed them from the lights, gave them water to drink, and sprayed their paw pads with water.

When it comes to heat, it goes without saying that you must never leave your dog in a car alone in hot weather, as the temperature inside a car is much hotter than it is outside. You likewise don't want to let dogs ride in truck beds that have been sitting in the burning sun. A standard rule to keep in mind is: "If it's too hot for your bare feet, it's too hot for your dog's paw pads." (Remember, too, that it's also not safe for a dog to be loose in a truck bed while driving.)

If you live in a climate with a strong winter and don't walk your dogs regularly during that season, ease into walking by building up your dog's stamina as the weather becomes warmer. We walk year round in four seasons where I live, but even so, when the summer weather comes, I walk the dogs either early in the morning or at dusk when the sun is not as hot.

It is also our responsibility to keep our dogs and children safe, especially when the two are together. People often think it's cute to have dogs interacting with small children, going so far as to assign the dog the responsibility to watch the child. This is clearly not acceptable. The preponderance of photos and videos on social media of dogs and children can perpetuate that mindset, despite the fact that many are endearing and appear to be safe for both the dog and the child.

Of particular concern are those that display a child creating physical stress for the dog, like in jumping on the dog repeatedly or attempting to ride around on him. You almost always hear adults in the background laughing, commenting on how cute it is. But while most dogs want to please and will tolerate this, if you look closely, you can see the dog is not comfortable. He is demonstrating stress by the look on his face and/or by frequent licking. This is a recipe for trouble if left to continue to the point where the dog feels he has no choice but to react. If this occurs, you will have a good dog defending himself from a child simply being a child, and both can end up hurt. Sadly, the dog is always blamed, when pet parents are responsible for managing and preventing situations like this from happening at all.

I have two grandchildren, Dominic who's three and Leo who's one, and my dogs are six and ten. Even though both are therapy-trained dogs, I would never leave them alone with my grandsons. Children and dogs always need supervision; toddlers cannot be expected to behave in any other way than as small children.

Dominic has often gently reached out to pet one of my dogs, and when he gets excited, the gentle pat quickly becomes a hit; for Leo at his age, it's natural for him to pat aggressively as well. To prevent this from happening, I guide each child's hand, teaching him how to safely and respectfully interact with Jazz and Jive. My dogs depend on me to provide that guidance, and my grandsons depend on me to keep them safe. Dominic's and Leo's excitement easily excites my dogs, and when that level for both escalates, it is critical to manage the situation, ensuring it doesn't get out of hand.

Despite the fact that both my dogs are very loving and protective of my grandsons – Jive will curl up next to Dominic or Leo and help him fall asleep, and Jazz is always within two or three feet of them to make sure everything is all right – dogs will be dogs and children will be children. We can't always predict how they may react to each other.

The Responsible Pooper Scooper

It may seem like a no-brainer, but when it comes to your dog's waste, it's vital that you pick it up regularly in your yard, and at all times during walks or outside activities. It's completely unacceptable to disregard this responsibility, not only for the public's sake, but for the health of your dog and others as well. With two dogs, I have to pick up poop every day – this is simply a reality when you have a dog (or two ... or more).

I'm consistently shocked by the number of people who don't pick up after their dogs; it is blatantly rude to leave waste on walking paths or streets. This disrespect only makes people more convinced that dogs cannot be allowed in public venues. With our goal being to take our dogs more places with us, we need to be responsible at all times to promote this concept. A small bag, and/or perhaps a wipe of some kind is all you need to carry. There are a variety of reasonably priced poop bag carriers you can purchase in the dog supply section of many stores. Dog owners owe that to everyone.

And if your life feels too hectic to maintain this responsibility at home? Believe it or not, you can pay someone else to do it for you. Some pet lovers actually have businesses where someone will come to your home daily – or on a determined schedule – and clean up your dog's waste. But in all fairness, tending to your dog's bodily functions is part of being a pet parent, and should therefore be an expectation when you bring a dog into your life.

Humane Treatment of Your Dog

I have great difficulty – and I know others do as well – with tying a dog to a stake or outdoor dog house and keeping him there most of his life. It's simply no kind of humane life for a dog.

Many of us have likely known of a dog in this situation, and it's incredibly heartbreaking. Dogs tied up all or the majority of the time have no ability to get any real exercise, have no contact with humans or other dogs, are unable to defend themselves well if any threat should occur, and can become depressed, lonely, and even perhaps neurotic. While keeping a dog chained in a yard is common in some parts of the country – and is even a traditional way of owning a dog for some people and cultures – there is simply no quality of life for the dog or the human to keep a dog tied up most of his life. In fact, it's downright cruel. Joy and love between a dog and a human can only come as a result of mutual respect and time spent together.

As pet parents, we have a great responsibility for the life of a beloved living creature. This is why it's essential to think the decision through wisely before making the commitment, one that carries with it thoughtful dedication of time, money, and responsibility. When you feel certain you can fulfill those commitments, do the proper research and know what your breed(s) require. The relationship you forge with your dog is priceless and will result in loving memories imprinted on your heart forever.

PATHWAY TO ADOPTION OR BREEDER

Life is better with a dog.
— AUTHOR UNKNOWN

The pathway you choose to find a dog is oftentimes a personal one. Many people are committed to rescuing dogs from shelters, while others are loyal to a particular purebred dog. Regardless of your affinity, however, both require appropriate consideration.

· · · · · · · · · · · Adopting Through a Breeder · · · · · · · · · · ·

What defines a responsible breeder?

Over the course of producing forty-eight episodes of *The Dog Show with Jazz*, I had the fortunate experience to work with numerous breeders, whom I carefully screened before agreeing to have them on as guests. My criteria was a love of the breed to the point where the welfare of the dog came before the profit; passion for their breed and commitment to preserving its health and well-being; dedication to breeding wisely, producing healthy dogs to carry the breed forward; and holding to strict criteria in placing a puppy. (While puppy placement is breed-specific, it almost always includes a thorough interview of the potential owner, their commitment to remain in contact with the breeder for a length of time, the presence of a yard, and other breeder-specific criteria I'll discuss shortly.)

Unfortunately, not all breeders today embrace the aforementioned qualities. Not only does it require commitment and hard work to find the best dogs to breed with each other, it takes diligence to find the best homes for the puppies. Not everyone is willing to put in this kind of time and caring, and that's why we must be aware of those who breed only for profit.

To begin, when working with a breeder it is a must to meet the mother – and, if possible, the father – of the litter. The mother should be at least two years old – three is even better – and you should visit the litter to see the mother interact with her puppies. If you can, I highly recommend you visit more than one time so you can observe her parenting skills as the puppies grow.

The breeders I worked with to bring Jazz and Jive into my family were all highly reputable and scheduled litter visits for all the potential human parents. When we came in, we were required to wash our hands and remove our shoes. Puppies this young are not vaccinated, and you therefore don't want to pass on any bacteria to them. Be wary if you have a litter visit and are not asked to comply to these guidelines – it's likely a red flag that the breeder isn't competent.

In my personal case, my breeder had interviewed me extensively and knew I was looking for a dog with a temperament to do Animal Assisted Therapy work. I had no small children, and I was working from my home with more time to devote to a young puppy. In our conversations, my breeder was constantly educating me about the breed and its needs.

Two weeks before we picked up our puppies, the breeder had a mini-conference – or "Puppy College" – in her backyard. All of us new human parents sat in lawn chairs as the puppies ran around playing, and we delighted in picking them up and giving them love. Members of the local Portuguese Water Dog Club spoke on grooming, veterinary care, social-ization, training, and nutrition, and they gladly answered questions. They also informed us that the club was available to provide ongoing support for new pet parents.

My experience was ideal, as it should be for anyone adopting from a breeder, but not all stories are as happy as mine.

Many people have a horror story about getting a dog they thought was healthy and from a responsible breeder, only to have the dog come down with significant health issues. In these cases, the breeder is almost always nowhere to be found or unwilling to take any responsibility.

My niece and nephew purchased a Rottweiler from a breeder who told them the dogs were "AKC registered," and even showed them the papers. This impressed my young niece and nephew, and they trusted the breeder to be ethical in large part based on these papers — so much so that they returned to adopt their dog's brother to complete their family. They were young, newly married, and now had two Rottweilers whom they fell in love with immediately.

Within the first three months, it became apparent that both had hip dysplasia, a condition that can be very painful for the dogs yet easily eliminated in the breeding process. Responsible breeders do not want to breed a dog with bad hips; in fact, they clearly state in the contract when you purchase the dog that the pet parent is required to bring their dog in for hip x-rays at two years of age, a cost the breeder pays for. This Rottweiler breeder not only bred unhealthy dogs, but she also took no responsibility for the hip dysplasia. My niece and nephew, now in love with the dogs, felt they had no choice but to find a way to pay for the expensive surgery to remedy the condition in both of them.

I hear stories like this over and over again. You may know of friends or family who have had similar experiences involving a dog's compromised health and a human's heartbreak at the hands of an irresponsible breeder.

Akin to this unconscionable practice is that of selling puppies online or to pet stores, which is something a responsible breeder would never do. These dogs are almost always raised in puppy mills — inhumane "breeding houses" steeped in cruel and deplorable conditions. While shelters advertise online, and you are able to go to the shelter and see the dog in person if you live nearby, puppy mills don't operate this way. As such, never purchase a dog online or in a situation where you cannot see the dog in person.

As a last note, if you choose to work with a breeder to find a dog, make sure you interview the breeder as the breeder is interviewing you. The American Kennel Club has a thorough list of guidelines for finding a responsible breeder. Do go to their website and view the entire list (see the Resources section for the AKC website).

· · · · · · · · · · · · Adopting from a Shelter · · · · · · · · · · · ·

To avoid the risk of working with an irresponsible breeder, you can always find a dog looking for a home in one of the many shelters nationwide. A shelter close to you likely has a website with a list of photos of all the dogs they currently have available.

When you are looking for a dog in a shelter, it helps if you can be as specific as possible about the dog you're seeking to bring into your life *before* you visit. There are so many loving eyes that will be looking at you, begging you to choose them, that emotions can understandably get in the way.

By discussing your needs and wishes with the shelter staff, you can obtain necessary information about the dog you are interested in. Also, as dogs are given health and temperament checks at a shelter, you will receive guidance toward the dog most suited for your situation, narrowing the number of dogs you meet. With the staff guiding the process for selecting and preparing your dog to come home with you, they will ensure your dog is healthy, that vaccinations are up to date, and that spaying or neutering is performed at the appropriate time. They will also instruct you on any other health issues your dog may have and how to care for them.

There are also rescue groups for most dog breeds. These groups work hard to find a lasting home for the dogs they have rescued, and you can find a list of them on the AKC website. Local shelters will be able to direct you to them as well.

·············· Ensuring Your Decision ··············

Obtaining a dog from a responsible breeder or from a shelter or rescue group are all viable options, but regardless of the path to adoption you choose, it's crucial to do your research beforehand. These are some questions you'll want to ask yourself:

- Do I want a large, medium, or small dog?

- Do I know what energy level I can best keep up with in any given dog?

- How much grooming am I willing to maintain? (If you want a dog who doesn't shed, for example, that will mean regular grooming because they have hair, not fur, and if it's not groomed regularly, it will mat and become uncomfortable for your dog.)

- Do I want a dog that will do well with children?

- Do I want a dog I can hunt with or one who can run with me?

- Do I want an older dog or a puppy? (Realize a puppy will initially take a lot more time and work, whereas a senior dog will come house-trained and likely bond with you right away.)

In considering all your needs and wants, you also want to weigh your living environment:

- Do I have an apartment, or a home with a backyard? (Dogs need space to sniff around and simply be a dog in a contained and safe environment. While having a backyard is ideal, smaller dogs and some specific breeds do well in apartments and urban living situations, as long as pet parents take them out to exercise in local parks or have indoor exercise spaces.)

- How many people are in my living situation?

- Do I have a family with children or is it only me?

- If more than one person will be living with the dog, is everyone in favor?

If even one person isn't on board with the commitment to having a dog, it will not have a successful outcome. I have seen this happen many times, as illustrated in the following story.

A young couple I knew was newly married; she (Mary) wanted a dog, and he (John) didn't but wanted to please Mary. After finding a great dog in a shelter, problems soon began. John tried to embrace the dog, but as he was only going along with having a pet to please his new wife, he and the dog never quite connected. In one situation, the dog bit John, which resulted in the dog being labeled as aggressive in his behavior. He demonstrated this aggressiveness with visitors as well by barking and charging at them. John and Mary then decided to keep the dog outside all the time. This not only didn't help, but it made the dog feel alienated from the humans in his life.

Fortunately for everyone, including the dog, a family member came to the rescue. She had a dog of the same breed and offered to take John and Mary's dog into her home. The two dogs immediately bonded and became fast friends, and the aggressive behavior and biting ceased.

While this is a story with a happy ending, it's also a cautionary tale. If everyone in the household isn't genuinely on board with bringing a dog into the family, disharmony will often emerge at some point. It's no different from when family members don't embrace other issues as a team, only with a dog, you have a sentient being involved who is relying on you for care. As such, integrating a dog into your home – whether you're single or have a family – not only requires research and thoughtful consideration of where and from whom you will acquire him, but regard for the dog as a valuable member of the family.

PART TWO

Essentials of Pet Parenting

THE IMPORTANCE OF SOCIALIZATION

All you need is love and a dog.
— AUTHOR UNKNOWN

*A*s we touched on in Chapter Three, we have domesticated dogs to live with us as companions. It is therefore our responsibility to train them how to successively live in our world — a world filled with sights, sounds, people, animals, and other dogs. A dog needs to be introduced to these experiences so he can live in our environment comfortably, which is why socialization is the single most valuable experience you can provide your dog.

Think about the effort you put into exposing your young human child to new experiences, new foods, new people, etc. Child development is a widely researched and published field that has provided us myriad ways to raise our children well; we expect to spend time and money helping them make the adjustments they require to grow up to be happy, functional adults. When human children are not afforded these opportunities, lack support within their family, or don't find guidance outside the family, they often have challenging life experiences. It's the same with our dogs. And because dogs will always encounter new experiences, we must view socialization as a lifelong commitment. The optimal time, however, is during puppyhood.

Socializing Your Puppy

With puppies, we have a window of time from three weeks to around sixteen weeks when they are most comfortable accepting new experiences. After that, it becomes more difficult – and even sometimes impossible – to help a dog expand outside their comfort zone.

One of the best ways to begin socialization is to enroll your puppy in a puppy kindergarten class. I know a certified pet and dog trainer who specializes in this training, and whenever I refer anyone to her class, they say that the training was not so much for the *dog* to learn, but for the *parent* to learn how to train their dog. We need training to be pet parents as much, if not more, as dogs need training themselves! Learning about socialization is a big part of puppy kindergarten and is typically a lot of fun for the parents and puppies alike.

A well-socialized puppy usually develops into a safer, more relaxed and enjoyable pet. This is because his world is bigger from the start, allowing him to feel more comfortable in a wider variety of situations than a poorly socialized dog. As a result, he is less likely to behave fearfully or reactively when faced with something new, such as unfamiliar people, dogs, or sounds. For example, a dog who is relaxed about car rides, honking horns, cats, cyclists, runners, veterinary examinations, and crowds is easier and safer to live with than a dog who finds these situations threatening. What's more, a well-socialized dog lives a much more relaxed, peaceful, and happy life than a dog who is constantly stressed out by his or her environment.

When people meet my dogs, their first comment is always, "Your dogs are so calm." After hearing it so often, I told my breeder, thanking her for such well-bred dogs. She smiled and said the breeding was only a small part of the picture, that the training I did with my dogs was the biggest reason they were so calm. In fact, members at dog club events would ask me – in jest – to take their dogs home to train them to be calm like my dogs. But the truth was that it was all about the socialization training I did with them when they were young.

My first experience socializing a puppy was with my dog Jazz. I trained him to be comfortable walking on a leash and took him on daily walks. During these walks, I intentionally focused on socialization by asking people we met if they liked dogs, explaining to them that I was socializing my puppy to new people. If they responded positively, I asked if they would be willing to pet Jazz. No one I met ever turned down the opportunity – most people love petting a puppy! If that went well, I asked if they would be willing to give Jazz a treat.

I used this same approach when we met someone with a dog. First, I asked the pet parent if their dog was friendly. If they said yes, I explained I was socializing my puppy to new experiences and that meeting a new dog would be very helpful. If they agreed, the dogs would meet and with the pet parent's permission, each dog received a treat. This was a positive experience for both dogs.

The bonus of this socialization technique was that I also developed ongoing "walking trail" friendships with other pet parents. When Jive arrived, I socialized her in the same way with these already familiar dogs and pet parents. It's been ten years now, and when we meet these friends on the walking trail, the dogs are still excited to see each other and the pet parents are delighted to greet and check in with each other. This is all a result of socializing Jazz and Jive as puppies. Though we have had to say goodbye over the years to some of our canine friends, we have also had the pleasure of greeting new ones.

On a recent walk, we met our neighbor's new nine-week-old puppy. Jazz automatically went into a down position to reassure the puppy he would be safe. Then Jazz, Jive, and the puppy all greeted each other by sniffing as dogs do. Now when we go by their house, the puppy wants to come and greet us. Because the pet parents encourage this, they are helping him become well socialized.

As you can see, socialization takes commitment and time. And while what I was able to do with Jazz and Jive as puppies was ideal, I realize not everyone has the time to do the same. So if you're short on time, a great way you can promote people contact with your dog is by hosting a party with your friends and family to have them meet your new puppy. As people arrive, introduce each person to your puppy, then let him frolic and play with all the people he has just met. Give thoughtful instruction to everyone on how to pet him, and even how to give him a treat. This will be a nurturing experience for your puppy, not to mention that your friends and family will get a dose of "puppy love."

Dogs who are well socialized are more comfortable with almost everything they experience.

As Jazz and Jive are both trained therapy dogs and have worked primarily with children, when we meet a child anywhere — especially on our walks — both dogs go into what I call "work mode." They seek out the child and want to greet him or her. What's more, if Jazz or Jive hears a child cry or scream (while playing), they both become concerned and want to make sure he or she is okay.

A word of caution, however: Even though my dogs are socialized, I still have to be aware of dogs being dogs. A big dog, although trying to be caring, can scare a child. Likewise, a dog passing us on our walk might exchange an attitude with mine, or mine with him, causing my dogs to react by barking and pulling toward him. (Not all dogs like each other and can give messages to each other with a look from a long distance away.) In short, when dogs don't know each other or a child is involved, it is critical to be extra aware.

···· Socializing Your Dog to Public Service People ····

Jazz was just a puppy when I took him to the local police department. I explained to the receptionist that I was trying to socialize my puppy to people in uniform and asked if there was an officer on duty who had a few minutes. She smiled and made a phone call. After about five minutes, I heard heavy footsteps – coming toward us was the tallest policeman I had ever seen. His leather holster squeaked as he walked, and he had a toothpick in his mouth as if he had just finished his lunch. He also had a big smile on his face as he said, "I guess I drew the short straw."

It took a few seconds for him to lower his long body to the ground so he could pet Jazz. I was so appreciative, and Jazz wagged his tail and enjoyed the experience. I think the officer enjoyed it as well. Don't be afraid to do the same with your puppy. If there's no officer available, they'll tell you, but the happy diversion is usually a welcome surprise if someone has the time.

Another great way to socialize your dog to public service people while on walks is to stop and greet city workmen wearing bright yellow and orange vests. Along with people in uniform, I also ask young skateboarders to let my puppies sniff their skateboard. Why? Because skateboards, bikes, and scooters often frighten dogs, simply for the fact that they move fast and make noise. When they encounter such a vehicle, letting the dog sniff the object helps him to not be so afraid of it.

For a comprehensive checklist of socialization experiences, you can't beat The American Society for the Prevention of Cruelty to Animals (ASPCA) website. The following table, used with permission by the organization, will allow you to keep track of what your puppy has been exposed to and at what age by placing a checkmark in the appropriate column.

Exposure Checklist for Socialization

Age in weeks:	8	9	10	11	12	13	14	15	16
Exposure to:									
Babies, toddlers, children									
Teenagers, adults, elderly people									
People with wheelchairs, crutches									
In-line skaters, cyclists, skateboarders									
Drunk people, people with odd gaits									
People in uniform, veterinarians									
Repair people, delivery people									
People with umbrellas, helmets, masks									
People with hats, beards, glasses									
People with parcels, capes, sacks									
People with strollers, wagons									
People of various ethnicities									
Kids at school grounds									
Crowds, clapping, cheering									
People yelling, loud speakers									
People dancing, singing									
Livestock, waterfowl									
Other puppies, friendly adult dogs									
Other pets									
Traffic, buses, trains, motorcycles									
Boats, jet skis, snowmobiles									
Manhole covers, grates									
Shiny floors, tiles, icy streets									
Gravel, cement, mud									
Revolving signs, swinging bridges									
Walks after dark, in bad weather									
Hot air balloons & airplanes									
Lawn mowers									

Elevators, automatic doors							
Balconies, stairs							
Drive-thru's, car washes, tunnels							
Electrical appliances, washers							
Vacuum cleaners, hair dryers							
Construction and machinery noises							
Wind, rain, thunder, snow							
Fireworks, sporting events, fairs							

· · · · · · · · · · · · Socializing the Older Dog · · · · · · · · · · · ·

We've been talking a lot about puppies and the advantages of starting socialization young. But if you have adopted an older dog, rest assured that all is not lost — socialization is still vital and possible; you simply need to be patient with your dog and willing to help him. Remember he may have had a challenging beginning with not enough love, attention, training, or proper care, so it's important to get to know his personality and his ability to tolerate new experiences. In doing so, note that you don't want to push your dog too fast; develop exposure to new experiences at a pace he can handle. Start with baby steps and gradually work your way up. If you have the means to do so, it is highly effective to hire a trainer who can help you. Overall, be willing to commit the time and effort to help your older dog adapt, learn, and feel comfortable in his environment. It will build the bond between you, and he will be more socialized and calm. A happy dog is well worth the investment.

Once again, socialization is lifelong training, so regardless of your dog's age, there are always opportunities to learn something of value.

I will never forget the day six-year-old Jazz met a tandem bicycle with two riders dressed in colorful bodysuits and big hats. This ordinarily calm dog became alarmed and began barking. He had been exposed to bikes, hats, and colorful clothing in the past — but never in one package, and it must have been too much at once for him. The bike didn't stop, and Jazz ceased barking after they passed us, quickly recovering from his initial reaction. But the lesson here is that every day of a dog's life can have an element of socialization to it, so try to anticipate what may be new for your dog whenever possible.

It's no surprise that establishing a relationship with a veterinarian is vital, and you therefore want to do this as early as possible. If you're feeling overwhelmed about whom to choose, breeders and shelters are wonderful resources, as well as friends who have dogs. Whether you're seeking a traditional veterinarian or one who has a holistic or integrative practice, the plethora of Internet reviews on veterinarians and animal clinics can be quite helpful as well. What's critical is yours and your dog's connection with the person you choose.

I, for example, was referred to a clinic where one veterinarian specialized in working with my breed of dog. Another vet at that same clinic assisted us in putting down our first Portuguese Water Dog, and she did so in such a supportive way for our dog and for us that trust became a cornerstone in my relationship with her. I have since found that I can ask her anything, and she will offer a thorough discussion about the options. She is likewise open to sharing her thoughts on articles I have read on dog-related issues, which is also an important factor for me. Having an open and trusting relationship and knowing you and your dog well are qualities you want in your veterinarian, so do what you can to build a good foundation for this relationship.

One of the first influential interactions your dog will have will be going to the vet for a general checkup, which should happen as soon as possible after he joins your family. Don't be afraid to interview one or more veterinarians to find a good fit for you and your dog – in fact, I would encourage it. Finding someone you can trust and talk to about your dog's health will be as important as the professionals you visit for your own health. Think about the criteria that is most meaningful to you (taking time to explain things, personality, willingness to educate, a holistic approach, etc.), and then ask for referrals or do some research to find at least a few good candidates. While a website may make a good impression and can be a great start, an in-person interview is always more definitive.

After the initial checkup, an annual wellness visit and routine vaccinations are typically all a dog needs. But once you have found a clinic and veterinarian you love, you can help your dog overcome any anxiety about going to the vet by taking her to the clinic when she doesn't have a scheduled appointment and letting her sniff and look around. Not only does this ease possible tension, it will also help socialize your dog with those who are waiting. Even with no appointment, the staff may be willing to facilitate your social visit (if they're able) by spending time petting and talking with her – and even give her a treat.

When you are with your dog in the veterinary clinic for a health visit, it is also important to set the tone for everyone involved. Be calm and breathe. Slowly pet your dog and reassure him in a slow, non-emotional tone of voice. Your dog will appreciate your effort to create a serene, nurturing environment for him during the experience, as will your veterinarian.

Having two dogs, I've found that when one has an appointment with the vet, I bring both dogs. That way they support each other, and one is going for the social experience, not for a shot or getting examined. As a result, they both smile and wag their tails when we go see our veterinarian.

When your dog learns that not every visit to the clinic will produce anxiety for her, it makes the visits less stressful for everyone involved. Your veterinarian will appreciate this as well. It is always easier to examine a dog who is not distressed about being at the clinic.

In sum, socialization opportunities abound; as pet owners, it's our job to be aware of them as they occur, each one offering the chance to help your dog feel more at home in a human world. When you give him every opportunity to learn in a caring environment – whether with other dogs and people or through activities – he will adapt better, react better, and be more peaceful and calm overall. Both you and your dog will reap the benefits.

Our Dogs Are What They Eat

Let food be the medicine and medicine be the food.
— HIPPOCRATES

holesome foods are as important for our dogs as they are for us. And just as there are a wide variety of experts touting the benefits of one human diet over another, the same holds true for our canine children. There are many people who are willing to give you advice about nutrition, and it often comes from their own personal experiences and opinions. There are also professional nutritionists emerging with well-researched data supporting their recommendations. The most important thing is that you know what is going into your dog's body and noticing how he or she reacts to that diet.

The basic diets for dogs available today are:

- Commercial dry kibble or wet canned dog food

- Commercial frozen raw or frozen dehydrated raw

- Homemade food, often based on raw ingredients

- A combination of any of the above

The current thinking is that a raw diet may be best for your dog. Not surprisingly, however, some veterinarians concur with this and others don't, making it challenging for pet parents to know what to choose. And while pet food companies will understandably promote their products, regardless of what's best for the dog, research now exists that explains the benefits of a raw versus a dry kibble diet.

We know that a diet of only dry kibble every day for a lifetime can be problematic for a dog. It would be similar to humans eating the same dry breakfast cereal, every meal, every day of our lives. Dr. John Tegzes, VMD, diplomate of the American Board of Veterinary Toxicology and professor of veterinary medicine at Western University Health Sciences, says:

> The results of a landmark study conducted by animal science researchers in California show that feeding a group of dogs a freshly prepared, whole food, lightly cooked, nutritionally balanced diet made from real food is scientifically shown to increase white blood cells and blood proteins that could benefit immune health.

Despite any conflicting theories that exist, it's clear that dogs need two things: a well-balanced diet and variety.

· · · · · · · Feeding a Well-Balanced, Healthy Diet · · · · · · ·

After doing extensive research to find the best food sources for my dogs, I have found the following to be excellent choices:

- dry dog food made with fresh-caught fish, and meat and poultry products with no antibiotics, hormones, or fillers

- raw patties of beef, chicken, or turkey made for dogs, with no antibiotics, hormones, or preservatives added (this can be combined with the dry food above)

- fresh fruits, vegetables, and other proteins like raw and slightly cooked organic ground turkey or chicken, salmon, or sardines (it's always best to provide organic whenever possible)

Because of the proliferation of commercial dog foods, we often forget that before the invention of dry kibble, we fed dogs only table scraps. Part of marketing the new dry kibble was to dissuade the use of table scraps or human food, saying it wasn't as healthy for dogs as the dry kibble was. While this has been a prevailing myth for decades, we have now returned to accepting the value of dog-safe human-grade foods as beneficial and nutritional for our dogs.

Jazz and Jive, for example, love fresh chicken, sardines, salmon, tuna, eggs, broccoli, cauliflower, carrots, peas, squash, bananas, strawberries, blueberries, apples, oranges, and any other human-grade food that is nutritional and not harmful to them. (Note that while fruits like apples and pears are good additions to our dogs' diets, you must be careful to avoid the core and seeds, which have a level of arsenic in them that is harmful to dogs.)

While this type of diet is ideal, you may naturally be concerned about cost; maintaining a raw-food diet can be expensive, so what do you do if this is outside your budget? Steve Brown, author and researcher of dog nutrition, says if you cannot afford a raw-food diet for your dog (which he recommends), you can supplement a dry kibble diet with human-grade food from your kitchen, like fruits, vegetables, eggs, sardines, and other like foods. I, myself, cannot afford an all-raw diet for two dogs, so I follow Steve's recommendation. I also feed both my dogs from an elevated dog food table. This aids in better digestion, and eating at this elevated height is a more comfortable position for the dogs.

If you *are* able to provide a raw-food diet for your dogs, even in part, Steve emphasizes the importance of making a homemade recipe right or not at all; raw diets often lack certain critical nutritional elements. In his book, *Unlocking the Canine Ancestral Diet*, Steve discusses this in detail. *Dr. Becker's Real Food for Healthy Dogs & Cats* by Karen Becker also speaks to raw diets for dogs and cats. In addition, the more unprocessed foods your dog eats, the healthier he or she will be.

········· · · · · · · · · · · Mixing It Up · · · · · · · · · · · · · · · ·

Variety not only keeps meals interesting for your dogs, but it ensures they're receiving varied nutrients. Here are some great tips I've learned as a pet parent:

- Rotate every bag of dry food you purchase – from beef, to chicken, to lamb, etc.

- Buy the medium-size bag, even if you feed two or more dogs like I do. The medium size will be eaten faster and will remain fresher. If a large bag of dog food sits for a long time, there is a chance that the bottom of the bag will become stagnant or even develop mold. This, of course, is not tasty or good for our dogs. (If you have more than two dogs and use an average of a bag of food per week, a larger bag obviously makes more sense for you.)

- Read labels. Avoid feeding your dog any food with a lot of fillers, which are ingredients like corn and wheat. Some believe these fillers can contribute to allergies in our dogs, not to mention they typically add no nutritional value to the food. And with the majority of corn and wheat today being grown as a GMO (Genetically Modified Organism) crop, it's vital to ingest only organic.

Another factor we all need to be aware of are food recalls, which can include treats and all forms of dog food. Two websites that provide a rating of all dry, wet, and raw dog foods and will email you information about recalls often before the news media announces them are:

www.truthaboutpetfood.com
www.dogfoodadvisor.com

As important as it is to focus on the *right* foods for our dogs, it's equally vital to be aware of foods that dogs should *never* eat. The following foods, which are listed on the Humane Society of the United States website, are harmful and can cause illness or even death:

- alcoholic beverages

- apple seeds

- apricot pits

- avocados

- cherry pits

- candy (particularly chocolate – which is toxic to dogs, cats, and ferrets – and any candy containing the toxic sweetener Xylitol)

- coffee (grounds, beans, and chocolate-covered espresso beans)

- garlic

- grapes

- gum (can cause blockages, and sugar-free gums may contain the toxic sweetener Xylitol)

- hops (used in home beer brewing)

- macadamia nuts

- moldy foods

- mushroom plants

- mustard seeds

- onions and onion powder

- peach pits

- potato leaves and stems (green parts)

- raisins

- rhubarb leaves

- salt

- tea (because it contains caffeine)

- tomato leaves and stems (green parts)

- walnuts

- Xylitol (artificial sweetener that is toxic to pets)

- yeast dough

Some people will tell you, myself included, that their dog consumed a food that was determined to be harmful for dogs and nothing happened. For example, Jazz once nabbed a couple of chocolate chip cookies. The small amount of chocolate did not have an effect on him, however, because of his body weight compared to the chocolate ingested. Another time he ate part of an oven mitt. I panicked and took him to the emergency clinic (at one in the morning!), and while I was waiting in the exam room, I read a long list of things dogs have ingested that brought them to the emergency clinic. There was no mention of an oven mitt on the list. The bits and pieces of the oven mitt were retrieved and all was well again. With much relief and many dollars later, we went home and both slept well.

Dogs will certainly find some of these "forbidden" foods (or other items) with their own opportunistic behavior. But before panic sets in, consider the breed, size, and amount of the food eaten; some dogs will not have a reaction. But since not having to worry about a potential health emergency is a good strategy for us and for our dogs, it's best to keep these foods out of your dog's reach if at all possible. It will save you worry, time, and money – and save your dogs from stress and discomfort.

We've touched on some of the healthy foods that provide balanced nutrition that dogs can eat, but here is a more detailed list of some of the human-grade foods friendly for canines.

Protein

Peanut butter is a great source of protein – there is actually peanut butter made just for dogs that does not have sugar and dogs love it. You can also use all-natural peanut butter for humans, but if you use one that's sugar-free, check the ingredients for Xylitol. I fill Kongs® (rubber toys used for play and training) with cut-up carrots and cover the opening with peanut butter. My dogs love it.

Other great sources of protein include cooked chicken, turkey, red meats, salmon, tuna, and sardines – and the fish have omegas that are good for our dogs' health.

Dairy

Cheese, cooked eggs, and yogurt are dairy products dogs really enjoy with meals or as snacks. Some dogs are lactose intolerant, however, and dairy is not good for them to ingest, so watch for symptoms of bloating, nausea, vomiting, or diarrhea. Yogurts also need to be free of added sugars and artificial sweeteners. (My dogs love scrambled eggs. I also give them their vitamin tablet wrapped in a small portion of cheese.)

Vegetables

Cooked or raw carrots, green beans, broccoli, zucchini, cauliflower, and even lettuce are tasty veggies for dogs. Jazz and Jive enjoy all these veggies (and when I need them to lose a couple pounds, green beans are a great filler to help them feel full when I need to cut back on other food for a short time). I buy frozen or fresh vegetables, organic when possible. As canned vegetables have sodium, they are best to avoid, if possible.

Fruit

Apples, bananas, blueberries, strawberries, raspberries, oranges, tangerines, watermelon, pears, peaches – almost any fruit in small amounts is good for our dogs (review the list of harmful foods on page 65 to remember which ones to avoid). I always add whatever I have on hand to their meals or as a snack. Just remember to avoid the pits and seeds of any fruits as they can be poisonous.

Other Nutritional Foods

Pumpkin is a good source of fiber as well as beta-carotene/vitamin A. It can help keep the GI tract moving and aid with digestive issues. I give both my dogs a tiny amount of pumpkin every day in their breakfast meal. This is especially helpful for Jazz, who is older – the pumpkin acts as a boost to his digestion.

Oatmeal is a great source of soluble fiber, as long as it is cooked and has no added sugars or other flavors. When I can't finish my portion of oatmeal at breakfast, I share what is left with my dogs and they always enjoy it!

Try these and other foods safe for your dog in small amounts at first. If she has any reaction, contact your vet immediately. Once you know your dog can handle these foods with no problem, introducing these nutritional options into her diet will provide nutrition and variety she will appreciate.

· · · · · · · · · · · · · · · · Feeding Theories · · · · · · · · · · · · · · · ·

As I discussed in Chapter Two, the alpha theory encourages humans to be dominant and the one in charge. One aspect of being in charge within this theory states that you should be able to take a dog's food dish away without the dog reacting. This is actually part of temperament testing for dogs in shelters. If a dog growls when his food is taken away, he can be viewed as food possessive or even aggressive. In all logic and reality, however, if you take food away from any species, they will be most unhappy.

Dogs who could be adopted pets are often euthanized for food guarding in shelters, but the ASPCA has released some heartening new research against euthanizing dogs simply for this reason, saying that an in-shelter protocol of free-feeding, combined with post-adoption support, helps keep food-guarding behavior from reoccurring in the home.

I know a successful dog trainer who says, "We mess entirely too much with our dogs' food. We need to just leave them alone and let them eat." I couldn't agree more. After all, how would you feel if someone took your food away from you while you were eating?

Dogs need to have security about their food. Often there is a history for a dog in this regard – he may have had to fight for food on the street or in his prior living situation. As such, training to help dogs overcome guarding of their food and food bowls can be positive for the dog and all concerned.

Yummy little snacks are something we can't seem to deny our dogs. As a result, pet stores are responding to consumer requests for healthy dog treats, offering a greater selection to pick from than ever before.

While treats are fun to give dogs, however, you must do so in moderation. Just as obesity is a growing problem for humans, it is also the biggest health issue for dogs. If we are indulging in junk treats (foods high in sugars and calories and with little to no nutritional value), we will likely give those same foods to our dogs. The result is often a weight problem for both the human and the canine.

For example, to avoid guilt while having a snack when my dogs give me the "you're having a snack so where's my snack?" look, I give them carrots and low-calorie nutritional options (which also reminds me to eat healthy snacks too!). Also, just as we don't need a snack every night, dogs don't need one either. You can try eliminating them on certain nights, or do what I do – have a "no treats after dinner" rule in my house, both for the dogs and for myself. (Don't ask me how I'm doing, but I will say the dogs are doing fine!)

Because I do a lot of training with my dogs, there are numerous treats involved. For this reason, I'm conscious of carrying treats that are organic or natural, low in calorie, and small in size. When I need to use a high-value treat in training or working, I use a protein like salmon or chicken. When I want to simply give my dogs a treat for no specific reason, I cut up carrots or small low-calorie foods and put them in a Kong®. As I mentioned earlier, I then spread some peanut butter over the Kong®'s opening. It's not only good for them nutritionally, but it keeps their mind and body occupied for some time as they search for the treat.

Another common item people give their dogs is rawhide chews or chicken jerky. These seem like perfect treats for dogs, but both are often processed and shipped from China or another Asian or South American country, where the processing of the jerky and rawhide often includes ingredients we don't feed our animals here in the United States. We are also not certain of the quality of the diets of the cattle and chicken used in the processing. Although the exact cause has yet to be completely determined, many dogs have died since 2007 from ingesting chicken jerky from China. As of January 2015, Petco and PetSmart pulled all chicken jerky treats made in China from their shelves.

When giving your dog a chew of any kind, make sure it is a product of the United States – and better yet, give them only sparingly, not at all, or by making it yourself using a recipe for jerky that calls for organic chicken. There are natural pet food stores that will be able to help you determine healthy treats, in addition to food for your dog.

When you are tempted to give your dog a treat, consider spending some time petting and playing with him or her, giving lots of verbal praise for being a good boy or girl. This is the best treat of all for your dog and for you. Just as humans sometimes eat because we're craving love and affection, our dogs can be craving our attention as well.

One of my favorite sayings is:

"Give your dog the best gift of all . . . your time."

Beyond that, use the guidelines in this chapter to keep your dog's diet balanced and nutritious, and focus on giving healthy treats, sparingly. Your dogs will benefit immensely.

EXERCISE: A MUTUALLY BENEFICIAL ACTIVITY

If your dog is fat, you aren't getting enough exercise.
— UNKNOWN

You may have heard the saying, "To lose weight, one must eat less and move more." It makes sense that the adage applies to humans, but it applies to animals too, especially with obesity being the biggest health concern for many dogs. In short: No more couch potato.

Walking my dogs is my primary form of exercise. I have walked Jazz almost daily (barring health issues and inclement weather) for the last ten years. When Jive joined our family six years ago, she naturally joined us. Not only am I fortunate to live in a place that has several beautiful walking trails, it feels good to move my body and see the dogs enjoying the exercise. It is also wonderful to connect with nature.

My dogs get a lot of exercise chasing and playing with each other in our backyard, but when I take my dogs on walks, their world becomes bigger. They get to smell new places – sniffing is the primary way dogs learn about each other and their environment – and expand outside the realm of our house and backyard. I always say Jazz reads his doggie newspaper by sniffing the boulevard to learn who has been where.

 Weather Considerations

We discussed weather in Chapter Three when talking about safety for our dogs, but it bears repeating here: When it is too cold or too hot for me, it is for my dogs as well. I happen to live in a state with extreme weather; you may live in a more temperate climate. In either case, it's best in hot weather to walk in the early morning hours before it heats up or at dusk as the day is cooling down. In contrast, in the colder season, it's best to take your dogs out when the sun is at its highest and the temperature is warmest. And while many believe that a dog's natural coat is enough to keep him warm in cold weather, this is a myth. In excessive cold, outerwear is worth the investment for your dog's comfort. Most dogs don't mind wearing a coat, and they soon realize it keeps them warm.

Another way humans and dogs are similar is that dogs' paws are not that different from our feet – they cannot withstand severe heat or cold. As such, doggie shoes or boots are another good investment for more extreme weather conditions. They may be hard to get on, but after initial resistance, dogs will tolerate and even likely enjoy how they protect their paws from either heat or cold.

As for weather-related physical conditions, heat exhaustion is real and can happen quickly for dogs in hot weather, as can frostbite in frigid weather. On nice summer days after returning from a walk, for example, my dogs want a cold drink and a cool place to lie down. When they're in the backyard on cold winter days, they will often raise their paws off the ground, signaling I need to call them in. Dogs are aware of the temperature and will tell you they need to come inside if it is too hot or too cold. When the weather is favorable, however, they should be outside playing more than they are in the house, if at all possible.

· · · · · · · · · · · Providing Indoor Exercise · · · · · · · · · · ·

Because of weather that prevents them from enjoying an outdoor walk and because many dogs in competitive sports train like an athlete, some people successfully teach their dogs to walk on a treadmill. Handlers want to keep their canine athletes in good shape, and they may not be able to walk their dogs the desired distance a treadmill could accomplish. In either case, consider taking turns on the treadmill with your dog. And if you're unsure how to train her to walk on it, you may want to hire a trainer to help you.

To expand on the treadmill concept, canine gyms are now opening, which are particularly great for those without backyards. These privately owned and trainer-supervised gyms allow dogs to work on treadmills and balance beams, and to run through tunnels and other agility equipment. While doggie gyms are just beginning to develop and may not be available in your area as of yet, no doubt they will be in time.

Whether you choose meandering about the great outdoors or working out at indoor facilities, the important thing is to physically move with your dog. Start with short distances and work your way up to ranges you both tolerate well.

· · · · · · · · · · · · · · · · · Backyard Space · · · · · · · · · · · · · · · ·

🦴

Aside from regular walking, I truly believe that every dog needs his or her own backyard – a place to move about freely and sniff out the critters (rabbits, chipmunks, etc.) that roam about. Just like us, they need a space to call their own, a space that allows them to run and play, even if only with themselves.

I am fortunate to have a large backyard where Jazz and Jive cannot only run freely, but where I can spend time with them too. For example, when I bring my camera into the backyard, they begin to run and put on a show. Granted, I take their pictures a lot and that may be their way of posing. All I know is that we have fun and I usually get some great shots. If you're not inclined to photograph your dogs, playing fetch or simply sitting with them is another great way to spend time together in the yard.

Jazz and Jive enjoy running and playing with each other for long periods of time in nice weather, as most dogs do when given the opportunity. They have their own way of interacting – they may vocalize and chase each other, appearing to be aggressive, but that is how dogs often play. What is important is to keep the play from accelerating to a high level that can get out of control. If you're able to supervise your dogs' playtime outside, which is recommended whenever possible, it's best to make sure they don't get hurt or into any trouble. Most dogs who are familiar with each other, like Jazz and Jive, have a good sense of the play level between them, but it's always a good idea to keep an eye out.

I remember a time my husband thought Jazz was being a little rough with Jive, so I decided to intervene, which is something I had never done before. After balancing the situation, Jive immediately moved in and nipped Jazz in his private parts. This is when I realized that my intervention was not needed; dogs can often take care of themselves.

While we are fortunate that Jazz and Jive's bond is very special – they have always been appropriately protective of each other and playful together – I do know people with multiple dogs who don't get along very well, so they are always supervising to make sure the behavior is appropriate and the dogs are not at risk of hurting each other. Depending on the situation, engaging a professional trainer to help with dog incompatibility issues may be necessary.

· · · · · · · · · · · · · · · · · Dog Parks · · · · · · · · · · · · · · · · ·

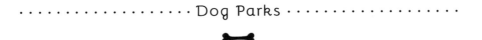

As not everyone has the luxury of having a backyard, dog parks and dog beaches can be a great alternative to allow your dog to exercise and stretch their play muscles. A dog park provides physical and mental stimulation for dogs that can only be experienced off leash. It also allows them to meet other dogs and figure out how to interact with each other socially.

Dog parks exist all across the country, so depending where you live, you will likely have access to one. I have personally only taken my dogs to a dog park once, and we had no problems. What was interesting was observing – I thought my dogs were active until I saw some particularly lively dogs at the park, running nonstop to burn off excess energy. I also observed that it was a social time for both the dogs and the pet parents. Some seemed to know each other from past dog park visits, and their dogs interacted well with each other. Situations like this can lead to future play dates for the dogs which is great for both dogs and humans. In addition, I overheard pet parents discussing the different types of dog breeds represented, and some were asking questions to learn more. As this was a great opportunity for education, I chimed in to share some information about my dogs that I hoped would be of help to other pet parents.

While my one-time experience at a dog park was mostly positive, I did walk away with some concerns I believe are important to point out. First, there is the realistic possibility of reactive dogs at the park. To illustrate, on one of my walks with Jazz and Jive, we met a lovely man with two golden retrievers. He was friendly to me, and when I asked him if his dogs were friendly, he said both were until a recent dog park incident where one of his dogs was attacked and is now frightened of unfamiliar dogs. Because it was not a good experience, he told me will not be going back to the park with his dogs.

While there is no guarantee such a thing will happen to your dog, there's also no guarantee it won't. Many pet parents don't realize their dog is aggressive until it is too late, running the risk of contributing to physical harm to people and other dogs, and possibly being open to a lawsuit.

In a dog park, I am especially concerned about the disparity in dog sizes. If small dogs are running with big ones, there is no way of protecting the smaller dogs. For this reason, I believe dog parks should adopt specific times or areas designated for small dogs, with a similar designation for large dogs. If you're able to suggest this type of arrangement in your local dog park, remember that voicing concerns can go a long way in effecting positive change that can avert potential problems or injuries.

My second concern was that the park I attended was fenced only on three sides, with a cornfield lining the remaining side. This was a clear safety issue for me. Certainly dogs can get lost in cornfields, which would be devastating. Any space that isn't confined by fencing or walls where dogs run free should be of concern, making that a factor when you choose a dog park.

Third, we can't deny the concern of canine diseases. I once planned a film shoot for my TV show and was looking for an outside space. When I suggested a dog park, my guests, who were bringing their dogs to the shoot, refused to go because they were worried about the possible exchange of diseases. As a result, we chose another more suitable location. As a pet parent, this is a valid concern. You don't know how other dogs are cared for, and it certainly would not be wise to bring a puppy not fully vaccinated to a dog park.

On the flip side, I recently became aware of private dog parks, situated on privately owned land and accessed through a membership fee. Members must adhere to structured guidelines, such as providing proof of current vaccinations, and all dogs must be spayed or neutered. All dog breeds are allowed; however, if a dog demonstrates aggressive behavior, he is asked not to return. And an added bonus is that there is human supervision at all times, enhancing the safety for both dogs and humans.

Of course, it should go without saying that all dog parks – public or private – require pet parents to clean up after their own dog. In some areas, the fines are hefty if you forget to do so.

In a perfect world, I would have a set of requirements for all dog parks, public or private. These would include:

- The availability of disposable bags for dog waste and containers to deposit it in.

- Information and rules posted and clearly visible.

- The park securely fenced in on all sides.

- Fresh water for the dogs to drink, and water for the dogs to wade in to keep cool on warm days. Fountains for dogs to run in would be a wonderful bonus.

- A sectioned area for small dogs less than twenty pounds.

- All dogs current on vaccinations.

- Areas of shade for the dogs and their pet parents. Both need protection from the sun on hot days.

- Volunteer or paid supervision to ensure safety for dogs and humans.

- All dogs required to have basic training and able to respond to a call like, "Fido, come."

- Everyone has fun and respects each other, dogs and humans alike.

While dog parks are not a good fit for Jive, Jazz, and me, I believe they do satisfy a need that many dogs and their owners have – a place to exercise, socialize, and have fun. I have many friends with dogs who love the dog park they attend and highly recommend it to other pet parents. Choosing the right park for you and your pet is key. Climate certainly plays a role: beach dog park areas are great for those who live by the ocean; hiking trails, lakes, and large ponds are nice offerings in other geographic locations. While many of these areas are not officially dog parks, they allow dogs access, sometimes off leash. The important thing is to have fun together, be aware and respectful of other dogs who may be present, and exercise at the same time.

· · · · · · · · · · · · Doggie Day Care Programs · · · · · · · · · · ·

If you are working full-time and need a place for your dog to be a dog while you are gone, doggie day care programs could be a good choice for you. One of the most common problems pet parents share is their dog destroying things when they're away from home. When dogs are left alone and become bored, destructive behavior is often a result. This problem can be resolved by changing the environment and providing interaction and play in a doggie day care program.

In addition to basic day care, high-end facilities are springing up across the country. In these hotel-like environments, dogs are pampered and treated to private suites with gourmet meals, as well as grooming, training, and boarding options. This of course comes at a higher price – depending on the facility and the options you select for your dog, it can be in the hundreds of dollars. While day care is often their primary focus, however, they will typically offer reasonable rates for day care alone without all the perks. For example, I know of a local high-end hotel for dogs that charges $28 for a full day of care, with various packages that have price breaks. Depending on what you want to pay, almost all day care programs are in the $8–$35 a day range. Note that pet parents are required to bring proof of vaccinations prior to beginning the program.

Another perk of doggie day care facilities is that they usually offer indoor and outdoor exercise areas. If it is too hot or too cold, they have air-conditioned or heated exercise areas inside. On temperate days, the dogs can be both outside and inside for activities.

In my experience, another positive was that the staff, who knew dog behavior well, supervised everything and eased the dogs into various activities gradually. They watched over dogs who were shy and kept them from more assertive dogs, while they kept smaller dogs under twenty pounds in another area specifically for them.

To provide him with fun and exercise while I was working, I first brought Jazz to day care when he was three years old. When I dropped him off, he was eager to get into the play area with the other dogs. When I picked him up, he was glad to see me and was tired. I was told he played with other dogs and had an overall great experience.

When Jive came into our family, I waited until she was about six months old to send her along with Jazz. Both she and Jazz played well together and with other dogs; however, after a time, Jazz played less with other dogs and focused more on Jive. After a few months, the staff told me they only played with one another, so I decided to stop taking them, as they were no longer deriving the benefit of day care. They could play with each other at home just as easily — and for free!

As doggie day care programs are still relatively young, we are only now beginning to gather data on what is working well and what concerns exist. We do know, however, that they are excellent for dogs under two years of age. It allows them to socialize with other dogs and get a lot of exercise, which meets their developing needs as puppies. Older dogs, on the other hand, don't need to play all day; in fact, the environment can be over-stimulating and stressful for them. As much as dogs enjoy playing with other dogs and being in a different environment, too much of a good thing can be a problem, causing certain dogs to be reactive or withdraw. In this case, they need some down time in the solitude of their familiar home environment, where they will re-energize and be ready to play again. If you are someone who works full-time and you want to leave your dog in the most beneficial environment possible, consider mixing doggie day care days with leaving your dog home other days, with a pet sitter to exercise him.

When I have to be gone for a long period of time during the day, I have a pet sitter who comes in and not only walks Jazz and Jive, but lets them run in the backyard as well. She also plays with them in the house and gives them a treat before she leaves. This arrangement is perfect for us

— Jazz and Jive are able to stay in their familiar environment, and they get to keep each other company and get the exercise they need. My pet sitter has developed a relationship with my dogs, and they enjoy their time with her. The entire experience is comfortable for Jazz and Jive, which of course is most reassuring for me.

As not all doggie day care programs are equal, you'll want to look for one that meets your needs and the needs of your dog. Trust your gut. If you observe anything about the program that does not feel right to you, make a note of it and seek out another option. It is also important to research and interview pet sitters to find the best one for your situation. Professional pet sitters go through a rigorous certification process to be able to enter your home, and most will have you sign liability agreements before working with you and your dogs. If a pet sitter is out of budget or you can't find one you and your dogs bond with, a good and trusted friend, neighbor or family member may also be ideal to walk your dogs for you when you cannot. There are a variety of resources today that can accommodate your changing needs, so explore what's best for you, and again, trust your intuition.

· · · · · · · · · · · · · · · Mind Games · · · · · · · · · · · · · · · ·

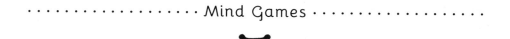

Excess energy and boredom are common problems for dogs. Being left alone for any length of time, especially long days, with nothing to do creates physical frustration and mental boredom. Mental stimulation is as vital a form of exercise as physical exertion, and many sports and even tricks and games will provide a level of mental stimulation for a dog. I highly recommend purchasing doggie puzzles as I have for my dogs to specifically engage their brain as well as their body. These puzzles and other games are created to give dogs a fun time trying to figure out how to get a treat.

One of the puzzles I have is a beginner-level game of "Spinner." Jive loves this puzzle, which is a wooden round cover with only one hole that when rotated, reveals an opening holding a treat. She has to spin the cover over each opening until she gets all the treats. Jazz's favorite is an intermediate-level puzzle where he has to slide wooden bars to reveal the treats. My grandson loves filling the puzzles and watching the dogs work them. A Kong® or any toy that holds food or healthy treats like carrots or apples can keep a dog busy physically and challenged mentally.

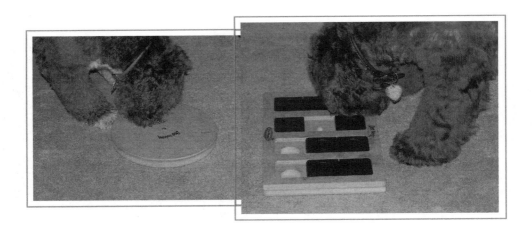

A few of the many sports for dogs that will provide physical and mental exercise include K9 Nose Work, agility, flyball, tracking, earth dog trials, water trials, and dock dogs (see Chapter Ten for more on these activities). Games like "find it" or even fetch or Frisbee are other great ways to provide both physical and mental stimulation.

Toys also provide frequent engagement. My dogs have so many toys that I need to swap them out on a regular basis to keep them new and interesting, but because they have so many objects to call their own and to keep them happily busy, they have no reason to get into my things. (If you feel like your house is being taken over by dog toys, you can simply bag up a bunch and put them away for three or four weeks, then bring the bag out and rotate them. This keeps old toys appealing and saves on needing to buy new all the time!)

While my dogs have plenty to keep them occupied, I don't tempt them with easy access to items I don't want them to get into. They are avid counter-cruisers, for example, so my kitchen counters and tables are free of anything of interest to them. (In the past I have lost a pan of lasagna and a pumpkin pie, to mention only a couple food items that went missing.) We have to remember that dogs are born opportunists, so where there is a will, they will find a way to a mouth-watering treat. It's best, therefore, to keep temptations hidden away.

When we make a commitment to keeping our dogs physically and mentally fit, we are fulfilling one of our many responsibilities in caring for them. Not only do we benefit from the exercise and engagement with them, but the safe and fun environment we provide for our dogs makes for a happier, healthier environment for all family members.

A Clean Dog Is a Happy Dog

There is no psychiatrist in the world like a puppy licking your face.
— Ben Williams

Dogs need us to help them maintain a healthy state of being. There are several ways we tend to these needs, but bathing and grooming are certainly two of the most frequent and critical.

A typical concern I hear from people with dogs is with regard to shedding. While certain breeds shed more than others, my groomer contends that shedding is minimized from routine bathing. There's even a special treatment that lessens shedding, which many groomers provide.

While bathing a dog can feel overwhelming for some people, especially if you have a large dog, we must think of the responsibility with as much importance as we do in bathing ourselves. Dogs count on us for this hygiene maintenance, and while not all dogs happily trot into a bath, we can't neglect this need. A clean dog simply smells good and feels good!

The frequency of bathing will depend on the dog and your lifestyle. If your dog is large with lots of fur, bathing him may be more of a challenge, so a monthly bath may be the desired frequency. It's up to you as a pet parent to determine a routine, and your groomer can also help you decide on the optimal bathing cycle for your situation.

There are three ways to keep your dog clean and feeling great: bathing him yourself, taking him to a groomer, or having a mobile groomer come to your home.

If you take grooming into your own hands, you must first consider the comfort of your pet. I know people who have active dogs with shedding coats who give their dog a bath with the garden hose in the backyard. Using cold water this way is quite uncomfortable for the dog. With this in mind, and knowing that bathing can be a challenge for pet parents, here are some practical tips to be mindful of when you bathe your dog:

- Most dogs resist having a bath, but you don't want to chase your dog to capture her physically or wrestle her aggressively to the bath area. It is best to calmly coax her with treats to the area you will be bathing her in.

- Do not use cold water. This will only create more stress for your dog. Use warm water and avoid extreme water pressure, as this can also be uncomfortable and stressful for him.

- Use shampoo and conditioning products that are specifically created for dogs' skin and hair. Human shampoo products are not recommended for use on dogs.

- Bathe your dog in a quiet, low-stress environment. Use a calm voice and supportive words throughout the experience. Talking to your dog, without yelling, truly does lend to both you and your dog having a nicer bath time.

- Many dogs can air dry in warm weather outside or inside the home. Dogs like mine that need to be brushed out, however, are often best dried with a dryer. Human hair dryers can work, but they can be too hot or take a long time to dry the hair. If you dry your dogs often the way I do, investing in a professional dog hair dryer may be the best solution. These dryers blow a more constant, acceptable heat for the dogs.

- Reward your dog with a nice treat after the bath. He has earned a payoff for cooperating in the bathing experience.

While shedding is a real concern for many pet parents, there are also dogs, like mine, who don't shed. Although this may sound like a perk of the breed, the truth is that they actually need to be bathed and groomed more regularly than shedding breeds. This is because they have hair like we do. If I don't brush the hair regularly, it mats; if it is not washed regularly, it smells. And because my dogs do a lot of therapy work, they need to be bathed every two weeks.

I take this responsibility seriously, and as such have a room in my home complete with a grooming table, professional doggie dryer, special scissors and brushes, shampoos and conditioners, and products devoted to bathing, drying, and brushing Jazz and Jive in between grooming appointments. If it sounds like a lot, it is. But it's one more reason to do thorough research on the needs of a breed before you decide to bring a dog into your life.

To keep Jazz and Jive in top form, I take them to a professional groomer every six to eight weeks, and I care for them myself in between. As our groomer says, "A clean dog is a happy and healthy dog." In addition to bathing my dogs, she also cuts and shapes their coat. Portuguese water dogs, like other specific breeds, need to be cut a certain way to adequately represent the breed. I can maintain the cut, but I need a knowledgeable groomer to set it properly.

One perk of bathing your dogs yourself and attending to them regularly through grooming is the opportunity it gives you to spend time examining their bodies for any abnormalities, such as any significant changes in the coat, skin, ears, etc. A good groomer can also be a partner in keeping your dog healthy.

The last time I brought Jazz to the groomer, she informed me that she found a small lump on him. I was aware of this and had already had our vet look at it. I thanked the groomer and told her I was pleased she noticed and appreciated her telling me.

Groomers often find concerns before we do, especially if you don't groom your dog yourself. But even if you don't bathe your dog, brushing her frequently allows you the opportunity to discover any obvious ticks, abrasions, or other health concerns. If you find something you think your vet should look at like a growth or cyst, it may be completely harmless or it could be a potential problem – discovering it early can ensure it's resolved sooner than later. Brushing is also a wonderful way to spend quiet, relaxing time with your dog.

If you go the route of using a groomer, either between baths and brushing you do yourself or for all your dog's hygienic needs, be aware that grooming costs vary by the size of the dog. According to Angie's List, you can expect to pay between $30 and $50 for standard grooming, and closer to $100 for additional services. The condition of the dog's coat is also a factor. If the coat is matted and requires a lot of work, the cost can be more as well.

Ear Health

Ear infections are common for dogs and can often be prevented with regular cleansing of the ears. Bath time is a good time for this, but if you don't bathe your dog, you can check the ears anytime by simply lifting the flap and/or looking inside the ear. If you know what to look for, you can use a small pencil-shaped flashlight; however, I rely on my vet to determine anything serious. I also use a gentle ear wash to keep the ears clean, which is a good product to have on hand at all times.

When dogs love each other a lot, they often express this love by licking the inside of each other's ears. In the dog world, this is a way dogs communicate affection. But as in the case with my dogs and any who have floppy ears, bacteria can grow quickly underneath and cause an ear infection.

Jazz was four years old when Jive arrived and had never had an ear infection. Now I keep medication on standby and wash the ears often to prevent a possible ear infection, courtesy of Jive's love for him.

TO CLEAN YOUR DOG'S EARS:

1. Hold the ear and gently pull up and away from the ear canal.

2. Squirt in the cleansing solution according to the instructions for the amount and gently rub the ear until you hear a swish sound, which alerts you that the cleansing solution is where it needs to be.

Note: You can purchase ear wipes for dogs to clean the external ear area, but using a liquid cleaner will get deeper into the ear canal and clean the area you cannot see or reach with a wipe.

· · · · · · · · · · · · Mani-Pedis for Our Pets · · · · · · · · · · · ·

You may be surprised to learn that if a dog's toenails are not trimmed regularly, they can grow too long and curl under. This can not only make walking difficult, but it can create serious problems for the dog. For this reason, keeping a dog's toenails trimmed is a must. And if you have dogs like mine who do therapy work, their toenails must not only be trimmed, but smooth, so that no one is scratched during their interactions with them. This is achieved by using a dremel, which is a tool that softens the nail edges after they are clipped.

Despite watching many groomers do this and being taught how to do it by my breeder — and I know many pet parents who do it with no problem — it's simply the one thing I have not mastered with my dogs. I can perform all other maintenance, but trimming toenails is not something I have been successful at or comfortable doing. If you're in the same boat, you can do what I do: take your dogs to a groomer every three weeks to have their toenails trimmed. While it's an extra expense, it's worth the peace of mind I have knowing their nails are trimmed well and safely. If you're a person who can trim your dog's toenails easily, just make sure you use good tools and have someone teach you who knows how to do it correctly.

While veterinarians and vet technicians also trim and dremel nails, they typically hold the dog down and restrain him, with one person holding and one person trimming. When I tried this with my dogs, it was stressful for them; they have been going to a groomer since they were puppies and are more comfortable standing to have their nails clipped. As other dogs may be more comfortable lying down and the vet experience is fine for them, what's crucial is determining what works best for your dog.

As with any experience for your dogs, remember to introduce the tools and the entire event of trimming toenails gradually and positively. If a dog has a negative early experience with this, it will take a long time to undo. As such, never force this activity, which will only create more resistance from him. This is yet another experience for your dog built on trust; you therefore want to build it, not break it. As trust is a huge part of our relationship with our dogs, enhancing it every chance possible is essential to building our bond with them.

· · · · · · · · · · Protecting Their Pearly Whites · · · · · · · · · ·

According to the American Veterinary Dental College, periodontal disease is the most common clinical condition occurring in adult dogs and cats, and while it is entirely preventable, by three years of age, most dogs and cats have some evidence of periodontal disease.

When humans don't brush their teeth regularly or have routine dental checkups, they too can develop periodontal disease. But because bad breath is often the only obvious symptom of it in dogs, pet parents don't always consider it to be serious, and therefore don't take action. In reality, though, bad breath is a symptom that something is wrong and a sign there is a need for dental attention for your dog.

We don't always see our dogs' teeth, but a routine vet visit can reveal everything from yellow and brown buildup of tartar along the gum line to red, inflamed gums. Tartar can also build up under the gums, eventually causing them to pull away from the teeth. When bacteria build up in these pockets of gum tissue, the result is irreversible periodontal disease, which is very painful for the dog.

Because of this risk, veterinarians and other dog experts are touting the importance of brushing our dogs' teeth daily to ensure good oral health. If this sounds crazy or impossible to you, I can assure you it's not … but it does require another level of time and commitment to your four-legged treasure.

I had the good fortune of knowing daily brushing was important when I brought my dogs into my life. As a result, I began brushing their teeth when they were nine weeks old. I started with a soft rubber cot on my forefinger, letting them sniff it and see it while I gently put it into their mouths and moved it around. Initially, I did this in short intervals; then, after they were used to that, I added some natural tooth gel for dogs to the finger cot. The intervals gradually extended in length, and I eventually introduced the toothbrush.

The way it works in our house is I brush my dog's teeth daily just after I brush mine. They have their own toothbrushes, holder, and toothpaste (I continue to find natural gel products specifically for dogs that work well and that the dogs like). At the time of this writing, neither Jazz nor Jive has had to have their teeth cleaned under anesthesia. If a medical reason arises that requires that procedure. I feel confident that my dogs will be fine, but right now my goal is to be as preventive as possible with my dogs' health. Brushing their teeth daily is a successful part of this prevention plan. And when my grandson stays with us, we all brush our teeth together. He helps brush Jazz and Jive's teeth, and that encourages him to spend focused time brushing his own teeth. Dogs and children can be good motivation for each other!

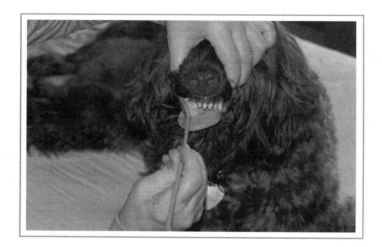

While beginning this routine with a puppy is ideal, many people adopt older dogs or have already been pet parents for years. If this is your situation and you want to introduce brushing, a first step is to ask your vet where to begin. Your dog may need a general cleaning under anesthesia to get most of the plaque off for a fresh start. It has long been believed that you have to bring your dog to the vet for a teeth cleaning, which involves anesthesia, and for dogs with dental problems, this is still a humane way of dealing with their teeth. After an initial visit, however, it's best to avoid putting your dog under anesthesia unnecessarily, which is why maintaining tooth care at home is ideal.

With an older dog, keep in mind that you will need a gentle hand, patience, and persistence, as well as a gradual introduction into the experience. Making sure you start with any issues diagnosed and treated will allow you to proceed with daily brushing to maintain prevention of future problems. Just like humans, some dogs build up more tartar and plaque than others, and some will have dental issues no matter what you do. The status of your dog's gums and teeth will dictate the necessary treatment, but daily brushing as a part of your dog's health maintenance program can only be a positive. What's more, a side benefit to looking inside your dog's mouth regularly is that you're able to detect any obvious problems early. An additional bonus is that when your dog allows you to put your hands in his mouth, it indicates trust in your relationship that will continue to build over time.

While bathing, grooming, and other hygienic tasks do require a commitment of time and money, any of these responsibilities you can perform yourself provides a great way to engage your dog with a caring touch and to spend time with him or her. All interactions with your dog are built on trust. As such, keep them positive and introduce them to your dog gradually, always with love and a kind voice. In doing this, you enhance your bond, and you'll both be happier because of your investment of time and energy.

PART THREE

What It Takes to Be a Super Pet Parent

TRAINING: An Overview

Folks will know how large your soul is by the way you treat a dog.
— CHARLES DURAN

Based on the statistics we have, the lack of spaying and neutering are the primary contributing factors to our dog overpopulation problem. These dogs often join the ranks of other dogs in shelters who, more often than not, end up being euthanized. According to the Humane Society of the United States:

> About 2.7 million healthy, adoptable cats and dogs — about one every 11 seconds — are put down in U.S. shelters each year. Often these animals are the offspring of cherished family pets. Spay/neuter is a proven way to reduce pet overpopulation, ensuring that every pet has a family to love them. Many cats and dogs who die as a result of pet overpopulation could have made wonderful pets.

It is obvious that spaying and neutering will reduce the dog over-population problem, but few people consider another huge factor that impacts this same growing problem: training.

When people bring a dog into their lives, training – as we've already mentioned – is often the last thing on the pet parent's mind; in fact, the percentage of dogs in the United States who are actually trained is extremely small. In a recent study conducted by the National Council on Pet Populations Study and Policy (NCPPSP) and published in the *Journal of Applied Animal Welfare Science* (JAAWS), researchers selected twelve animal shelters in the United States to observe for one year to determine why dogs and cats were surrendered. What they found was that ninety-six percent had no obedience training.

I remember three distinct times I had Jazz with me for therapy work at a children's hospital when an adult asked me, "Did he come like that?" The question surprised me each time, and I began to wonder if people thought dogs came programmed with trained behaviors. Unfortunately they do not.

When Breezer came into my life, I did some initial training with him but felt overwhelmed with the experience. At that time, I simply didn't understand the importance of training for a dog – I thought it was a nice thing to do but something I didn't have a lot of time for, not to mention I didn't have enough insight into what Breezer needed. Now, however, many years later, I have much more information about the importance of training a dog. And because Jazz and Jive have both had – and continue to have – a lot of training, it has made living with them a joyful experience. Other people can also enjoy being around them, and they are comfortable around people in various situations.

A great way to think of training is that it is preparing your dog to live in a human world comfortably and with respect. A highly regarded trainer I know says, "A dog who is trained will likely not be surrendered to a shelter." When we look at training from a pet parent perspective, we need to view training both as a dog's right and as our responsibility.

Consider for a moment that there are children who don't attend school on a regular basis and often don't live in a stable family situation. Many of these children are neglected and don't get the emotional support and parenting they need to feel comfortable in the world they live in. In seeking ways to cope with their stress, some hold everything in, some may not even speak, and others act out and have a hard time concentrating. All of these children feel stressed and uncomfortable in their world most, if not all, the time. Because their needs are not being met to help them develop confidence, they struggle to fit in, both in school and in society. Sometimes these children will receive help from another adult or even a community program, but many don't and struggle much of their life.

As responsible parents to our human children, most of us strive to provide the best developmental support and education possible throughout our child's lifetime; no one, if asked, would say their goal was to neglect their child as much as possible. Yet it happens. And as deplorable as that is, it can happen even more easily with pets. As accountable pet parents, the commitment to train our dogs must be a part of the responsibility we assume when we bring them into our lives.

You've no doubt been in the presence of an untrained dog – one who may be aggressive, out of control, anxious, fearful, hyper, or stressful to live with. When I'm walking with Jazz and Jive, we meet many dogs who jump and pull on the leash. This is not because they are inherently bad dogs; they are merely not trained how to walk on a leash or how to greet other people or dogs.

The reality of denying your dog training is that it creates a stressful life for him. Dogs live in an anxious and sometimes fearful state when they meet people or face new situations – *if* they have not been prepared for these everyday life encounters. If you want your dog to be calm and confident, you need to commit to training, and that means spending quality time with him. Once you make this commitment to your dog, you soon realize that training is a lifelong experience. Just as you support your human child through the various phases of life, supporting your dog in learning behaviors and coping abilities in new situations throughout his lifetime will enhance his quality of life – and yours.

Five key benefits to training are as follows:

- Your dog can accompany you with calm and confidence on walks, hikes, beach runs, and diverse gatherings with dogs and other people.

- You, your family, and other friends and visitors can enjoy being around your dog because instead of jumping and barking anxiously, he is happy and appropriately playful.

- A trained dog has the best chance of remaining in his forever home for his lifetime and not be surrendered for "out-of-control behavior."

- The training time you spend together develops your bond and nurtures your relationship. You become a team with the opportunity to pursue other activities if desired, such as sports for dogs, service, or therapy work.

- Your dog is grateful and loyal to you as his human partner and parent, giving him security and trust as he lives each day of his life with you.

· · · · · · · · · · · · · Training Techniques · · · · · · · · · · · · ·

As a pet parent, it is crucial to be at least somewhat educated about training, as techniques fall into two distinct categories: dominance theory and positive training.

Dominance training uses intimidation and fear to motivate a dog to learn behaviors, asserting that the human needs to be in charge and that the dog needs to be dominated to learn. To accomplish this, pet parents often use equipment such as prong collars, shock collars, choke chains, and other like equipment that will help create this form of dominance through physical pain for the dog. If it sounds cruel, it is. In fact, the dominance theory has come under scrutiny of late. Despite its widespread acceptance in certain circles, The Association of Professional Dog Trainers eschews dominance theory and supports the use of positive techniques in all training for dogs, offering a statement as to why on their website. (See the Resources section for more information.)

On one of our walks, I had an encounter with a woman and her pit bull that completely unsettled me. He was a beautiful young dog with a lot of energy, and the few times we had crossed paths, I noticed she always had difficulty managing him. On this particular day, her dog had a double saddlebag on his back with huge, heavy rocks in each bag. My heart ached for the dog and for his pet parent, and when we talked about it she sounded conflicted, telling me she had hired a trainer who told her to do this to control her dog's "out-of-control behavior." While she thought it was helping a little, I couldn't help but think of how the dog's bones were still developing, wondering what this heavy weight for long periods of time might do to him. As for the dog, he looked sad and confused.

Pet parents can be frustrated when their dogs behave in a way they perceive as mischievous or troublesome and feel at a loss about what to do. When they reach out to an expert for help, they often have no reason not to trust that expert guidance. But this is when you need to take a moment, step away from the situation, and ask the question, "What is the dog thinking or feeling about this?" Striving to see things from our dog's perspective is as vital as striving to put ourselves in other people's shoes.

In the scenario I just described with the pit bull, he was a year-old dog with a lot of puppy energy. He couldn't know how to act without devoted time from his pet parent helping him learn good manners and finding positive ways to run off his energy. Since a dog is unable to figure out what is expected from him, we must provide those expectations in a loving way. Dogs truly want to do the right thing, but they need assistance learning what that means.

Using fear and intimidation techniques that can inflict pain only creates aggression and fearfulness in a dog, which merely contributes to an existing problem and doesn't resolve the situation. On the other hand, training a dog with treats, toys, petting, and verbal praise each time he demonstrates a desirable behavior teaches him that the behavior will get him a reward of some kind, motivating him to perform it willingly. Using positive techniques is how I have always trained my dogs, and I recommend you do the same when training yours.

········ Four Criteria for Successful Training ········ Using Positive Techniques

Time

Understand from the beginning that training takes time. There is no magic technique that will make your dog a forever-happy, well-mannered dog in just a few minutes. As with teaching a child to read, solve math problems, or ride a bike, it requires repetition. When you begin a training or practice session with your dog, make sure you have allotted enough time in your schedule to repeat the activity a number of times. Experience will help you become more clear about what you can accomplish together in a given period of time. Beginning with five to ten minute sessions may be helpful to both of you. Scheduling two to three of these short sessions a day is a good way to begin your training experience. To this day, my training time with my dogs are always short sessions.

Patience

Training a dog is much like trying to converse with someone who does not speak our human language. Canines want to please us, but we both need to overcome the language barrier; physically hitting a dog or yelling at her is not the "language" to choose. Learning how to implement positive training techniques and making the time to do so requires patience. When you approach training with a patient frame of mind, you're able to get to know your dog's personality and learning preferences. For example, some dogs are motivated by food and some by toys. It takes patience to develop good communication and understanding in any relationship, especially with our dogs.

Fun

Training must be fun for you and for your dog; having a good time keeps you both in the game. If you or your dog become frustrated with the training experience, simply stop and try again at a later time – but make sure you end in a positive way by reinforcing a behavior you know your dog has successfully learned. Ending on a happy note always makes the prospect of returning more favorable for both of you.

Integration

It is critical to transfer your dog's newly learned behavior into day-to-day living. After you have mastered teaching your dog some of the basic behaviors like sit, stay, or come, you must integrate these behaviors into daily life. Think of it as teaching good manners to your dog.

For example, before you let your dog outside, ask her to sit at the door. Then open the door and release her from the sit, offering praise. When you give your dog a treat, ask her for a sit or a down, and then reward the behavior with the treat. You can do this when taking walks or practicing sits before crossing a street, rewarding the sit with a treat or a loving pat by saying, "good boy" or "good girl." Asking your dog to "leave it" teaches him not to take an item you don't want him to have, like your slipper or food.

After the desired behavior is well learned, you don't have to use treats all the time; treats often work best when training to learn a new behavior. My dogs, for example, respond well to treats and positive touch and communication, but after the behavior is mastered, random treats and verbal praise reinforce maintenance of the desired behavior. What's important is to practice these training techniques in a way that makes it fun for both of you. It will solidify the learning, and it will build your ongoing bond and relationship – not to mention that trained dogs are much more fun to live with!

You may have figured this out already, but dog training is really more for the pet parent than it is for the dog. When I attended my first training class, I didn't know what to expect. Like many people, I had the misguided notion that the class or instructor would somehow magically train my dog. I had no clue I would be doing all the work myself. I also didn't realize how great the rewards would be.

· · · · · · · · · Being in Charge in a Positive Way · · · · · · · ·

When training with positive techniques, it is important to determine a way for your dog to know when you mean business. Because dogs are attuned to our tone and body language all the time, creating a shift in either or both is the most effective. For example, when I need my dogs' immediate attention, I inflect a deep, low tone to my voice and straighten my body. While I am firm in both tone and facial expression, I'm not yelling, and both Jazz and Jive know this is a tone they need to acknowledge. This tone is different from the one I use when we are casually interacting, or even the one I use when we are in a training situation.

Not only is your dog's familiarity with this tone important for obedience, it can also save him from harm. When you need to get his immediate attention to keep him safe, you must be able to communicate in a way that he understands the urgency. Being dominant is not necessary; your dog already knows you are in charge of his food, exercise, and other basic needs. Establishing a tone and body language that says "this is important; you need to listen to me" confirms this level of respect and understanding.

· · · · · · · · · · · · · · · · · · Trainers · · · · · · · · · · · · · · · · · · ·

Now that you and your dog are ready for training, it is crucial to find a good trainer who implements positive training techniques. But how do you find a good one?

Trainers, like dogs, come in all shapes, sizes, and temperaments — and unfortunately, there are no established state, federal, or other universal guidelines for people who train dogs. In truth, anyone can put up a sign advertising they are a dog trainer, and what's worse is that there are no ongoing training requirements to keep them current and accountable. Although this can create a challenge for pet parents, the good news is that excellent programs have become quite plentiful these days that offer superb training for those interested in becoming a credentialed trainer — and these programs command ongoing education, accountability, and updated certification, much like those for teachers, police officers, fire fighters, counselors, nurses, and other professions.

When seeking a trainer, you'll want to verify that they have been certified by the Association of Pet Dog Trainers or the Certification Council for Professional Dog Trainers (see Resources section). Other qualified organizations may exist as well. These trainers who hold the title CPDT (Certification for Professional Dog Trainers) are required to obtain continuing education credits on a regular basis to retain their title. Although working as an apprentice with an established trainer has been the tradition and is still a common method of learning, the trend of acquiring formal training and accreditation is gaining favor in the canine community.

Despite credentials, however, trainers do vary in personality and professionalism, so if possible, see if you can sit in on a portion of a class to see how they interact with clients — or at least talk to someone who has worked with them to find out what they're like. If a trainer offers their first class for humans only — no dogs allowed — that is a sign the trainer realizes the importance of engaging with the pet parent specifically. It is also a good sign if a trainer is comfortable inviting family members to attend the class to observe and be involved appropriately.

I was once in a class where I was surprised and taken aback when the trainer actually laughed at all the participants for how we looked working with our dogs on a specific learning exercise. I have likewise been in class situations where the trainer spoke in a condescending manner to the participants, which created some tension from the beginning of the class experience. I think it is safe to say that a pet parent in a training class for the first time is there because they know nothing; they often don't know what to expect and can appear to be clueless. I remember feeling very uncomfortable and unsure of myself in my first several classes, which is why you want a trainer who will be compassionate and respectful to all involved.

Once you've found a good match in a trainer, the benefits of being with other pet parents and dogs in a class setting are numerous. One of the biggest benefits is socialization to other dogs and humans. Participants in a training class are often responsible adults with diverse jobs and families who make daily decisions to maintain their health, home, children, and financial status. But while they may feel confident in these roles, being a pet parent is usually a whole new world for them, and they can quickly feel like a fish out of water. These same people have often not dedicated much, if any, time toward understanding their four-legged addition to the family, and they've come to the class with the expectation that the trainer will magically make everything wonderful for them and their dog (remember I felt that same way once?).

Yes, this is unrealistic, but it's the mindset many new pet parents have. In a group setting, though, everyone has the opportunity to realize what they don't know, and it is a huge step for everyone, especially the dog. This is the time for a trainer to demonstrate their people skills and engage the human attending the class, not judge or talk down to them. Training for that clueless pet parent and their dog is lifelong, and it all begins with that first class. When the initial experience is positive, you are much more likely to return for subsequent classes.

My friend and trainer who invited me to her K9 Nose Work class is an example of a superb trainer. Because she has solid people skills and sound knowledge of dogs and the sports she teaches, I enjoy being with

her in class as much as my dogs do; I always feel respected and included in the experience of learning how to train my dogs while with her.

While there are great as well as poor trainers out there, I am
fortunate to know and work with many excellent ones. Although I have
had some unfortunate experiences with trainers, all of them have helped
me better understand that successful training for my dogs and for me
embraces training that employs positive training techniques. This insight
has guided me in every interaction I have with Jazz and Jive, which has
resulted in a rich and loving relationship between us.

If you live in a small town, finding a trainer who is geographically within
reach can be a challenge; if this is true for you, there are training programs
available on the Internet. The American Kennel Club has training modules
on their website, and trainers such as Ian Dunbar, who is a national, well-
respected trainer, offers many options on his website as well, including a
free download on how to train your new puppy. You can also access basic
beginning training for you and your dog through books, DVDs, or the
Internet. Just make sure the trainer and the techniques they use are positive.

· · · · · · · · · · · Red Flags to Heed in Trainers · · · · · · · · · · ·

Some trainers are people who profess they like being with dogs more than
with humans. While this may be a generalization and a sentiment many
people who have a dog may feel sometimes as well, this is not a desirable
quality in someone who needs to engage a first-time pet parent in an unfamiliar training class. Remember, the training is more for the parent than
the dog, so the trainer's ability to engage well with humans is paramount.

Another situation I have observed is when a trainer is burned out and/
or doesn't have a healthy outlet for their frustrations. It is understandably
disconcerting to constantly meet or work with people who seem clueless
about their pet parenting responsibilities, but many of us simply don't know

any better. While a poor trainer may find this to be a reason for judgment, an excellent trainer can view this ignorance as an opportunity to inspire the pet parent.

When I was a nurse and a therapist, it was essential for us to have client-centered meetings where we addressed challenging situations and shared skills and techniques — or learned new ones that could be helpful to each other. It was a professional environment and these best practices prevented judgment and gossip about clients. Let's face it: anyone in any profession is vulnerable to becoming "burned out." And because there is no professional group or structure in place to provide this kind of support for dog trainers, the individuals are responsible for their own professional behavior and well-being. A trainer who is experiencing burnout may not even realize it. As such, it is my hope that peer support and following professional guidelines will temper a trainer's tendency to take out frustration on a client.

Overall, trainers are committed to helping people train their dogs successfully, and like all professions, some are much more skilled than others. Also, because of the past focus on dominance training, it is important to know the philosophy of the trainer. For example, I know a trainer who says she implements only positive training techniques; however, when I attended her class, she taught some quite negative ones, like pulling a dog's head up as high as it would go, either by the Gentle Leader® or by the leash on the buckle collar, to teach him to sit. Not only did the dogs seem fearful or confused, but I as a participant was shocked someone would suggest doing this to a dog. Even more disturbing was that the majority of the participants seemed to trust her guidance. Again, when we don't know any better, we often follow the advice of someone we perceive as an expert, even when that advice may not actually be the best. This is why I recommend using the following checklist when seeking a trainer and working with them:

- Interview the prospective trainer, preferably in person, and don't be afraid to ask pointed questions about their techniques and background.

- Request to see their certification (which they should happily provide if it's legitimate) and verify that it's indeed legitimate (on the CCPDT website, for example, you can search for credentialed trainers by state), or better yet, look them up beforehand.

- Ask to attend a class and observe the trainer in action before you sign up for an actual class. While there, make sure you are comfortable with their training techniques and that you feel respected as an individual. If these criteria are not in place, look for another trainer.

- Ensure no physical aggression, pain, or distress for the dog are involved in the training.

- When you find someone both you and your dog feel good working with, discuss ongoing training with them to see what they suggest or offer. Remember: this person is training *you* to train your dog over the course of his or her life.

- If at any time your stomach feels tight, or you question a technique being used on your dog, trust that concern and raise it with the trainer. If you are unable to find a resolution, find another trainer. You are paying a fee to help you learn to train your dog, and that can only work if you feel a mutual respect and confidence with each other. A trainer with good people skills who can relate well to the human at one end of the leash as well as the dog at the other end is a valuable find.

Keeping all this in mind, it is also important for us as pet parents to have an open mind and a willingness to learn from the trainer. My trainer friends tell me their biggest frustration is a pet parent who is unwilling to move beyond excuses for their dog's behavior and take responsibility for their pet's training. As pet parents, we play a key role in making training successful for our dog, and we need to take responsibility for our part just as the trainer does theirs.

Now, let the training begin!

$\mathcal{G}$ETTING $\mathcal{D}$OWN TO $\mathcal{B}$ASICS

Dogs do speak, but only to those who know how to listen.
— ORHAN PAMUK, author of *My Name Is Red*

$\mathcal{I}$f you want to build the foundation vital for your relationship with your dog, you will need to implement some basic training. This training, as we've discussed several times, is a lifelong commitment, much like the years we spend in school or the dedicated time we spend teaching our children valuable conduct and skills. If you think of your dog's life as an ongoing educational experience, you will always remember that training — no matter how large or small the guidance — never ends.

Whether you have a new puppy or a rescue dog who just joined your family, it is important to begin building trust and a bond immediately. This will make the training experience more successful. You can do this by spending playtime and quiet time together, and by using a caring, gentle voice and touch. If your dog's name is new to her, be sure to use it often until she learns to respond to it. Develop your relationship to the point that she follows you and wants to be with you all the time. Once you have this positive base connection, you and your dog can begin your training journey with classes or one-on-one with a trainer.

· · · · · · · · Beginning Basic Ten Behaviors · · · · · · · to Teach Your Dog

1. **"Sit"**

   Asking your dog to sit is not only good manners, but it may also be a safe position for him to be in, like sitting close to you on leash waiting to cross a busy street.

2. **"Stay"**

   Asking your dog to stay (whether in a sit or a down position) helps your dog develop self-control.

3. **"Down"**

   A dog responding to a down request is trusting of his environment because it is the position that may make him feel vulnerable – he is not on his feet and able to run if necessary.

4. **"Come"**

   A dog who responds well to coming when called shows good discipline; this is also a behavior that could keep him safe, either from running away or running into a street.

5. **"Off"**

   Asking a dog to get off a sofa, a bed, or any place you don't want him to be is often necessary; a dog may be allowed on a sofa but may also need to get off when asked. ("Off" and "Down" are different but are frequently confused by humans, and therefore by dogs as well. "Down" means going to the floor in a lying position, while "Off" means moving off the object you don't want him on.)

6. **"Leave it"**

   I ask this of my dogs every day, especially on walks when we come upon something undesirable on the trail. I will say, "Leave it," and my dogs won't investigate any further. I use that phrase for anything from a dead bird I don't want them sniffing to something that fell on the floor that they shouldn't eat. It's important to note that this behavior could keep your dog from serious harm as well.

7. **"Hurry Up"**

I learned this from a breeder friend to tell my dogs to go to the bathroom. There are varying phrases or words for this purpose. Find one that works for you.

8. **"Paws Up"**

I use this phrase to ask my dogs to get up into or onto something, such as into the car, or onto a chair next to a client who is in a wheelchair (in Animal Assisted Therapy work), or up on the sofa at home.

9. **"Wait"**

This is more temporary than a "stay" – I use it, for example, when I am fixing meals for my dogs and Jive gets so excited that she begins to jump up and down. Asking her to sit and wait is therefore necessary.

10. **"Heel"**

This is the basic word for walking on or off a leash. Asking a dog to heel is telling him to walk with you.

It's important for us as humans to remember that our dogs need a specific word or phrase to associate with the behaviors expected of them. While it could actually be any word or phrase, choose one that makes sense and use it consistently to request the behavior associated with it. This sets a foundation for communicating with our dogs.

As I'm sure you can imagine, the earlier you begin this training the better. That means practicing at home and on walks, and incorporating the learned training into daily activities. Asking for sits and stays and calling your dog to come throughout your day will reinforce the practice of these newly learned behaviors; as a result, they become the norm in how you relate to each other and how your dog develops good manners and polite behavior.

If, however, a dog is fearful, very shy, or has other issues, training may not be enough. In this case, there are options available to help our dogs, such as Tellington TTouch® Therapy, Healing Touch Therapy, and Essential Oil Therapy, just to mention a few of the many alternative therapies available today.

· · · · · · · · · · · · · · · · · · Puppy Class · · · · · · · · · · · · · · · · ·

Puppy class is a means to begin learning basic behaviors, and it can be a lot of fun for dogs and pet parents alike. I remember going to my first class and not knowing what to expect at all. I was in love with my puppy and was trying to control his behavior as much as I could. Of course, he was resisting my control at every turn, and so we were beginning our training from this posture. I soon learned I had a lot of company with other pet parents attempting the same approach with their puppies.

I was fortunate to have an excellent trainer who recognized our effort to attempt to control our puppies but gave us specific guidance on how to do things more effectively. Her technique was based on having fun. For example, she taught us how to play a game with our puppies to make sure they knew their names, how not to bite and get rewarded for doing so, and how to begin walking on a leash. While these are only a few of the valuable things you will learn in a puppy class, the greatest takeaway I received was that we were there to learn how to train our puppy *as a pet parent*. I distinctly remember feeling a sense of responsibility upon hearing that, which was something I had not felt clearly before. At the same time I knew instinctively that I was in good hands with her guidance.

In most puppy classes, the real fun is at the end of the class when the puppies all play together. Because even puppies can vary a lot in size, it is important to have puppies of similar size play together and always with close human supervision. This encourages the socialization puppies need with other dogs, as well as with other humans. And in utilizing positive techniques, such as treats, play, praise, toys, and petting as rewards to reinforce the behavior you want your dog to learn, puppy class is the beginning of learning these basics to train your puppy with love and caring.

· · · · · · · · · · · · · · Good Manners Class · · · · · · · · · · · · · ·

An appropriate next step after puppy class is to enroll your dog in a good manners class, which is a great primer to set some strong foundational behaviors for lifelong obedience. In this class, you'll work more on the basic commands of sit, down, stay, and come. You'll also learn how to tell what your dog is communicating to you with *his* body language and how he reads *your* body language. For us, it was a time to focus on our newfound relationship with appreciation and fun, and it set us up perfectly for obedience class.

· · · · · · · · · · · · · · · Obedience Class · · · · · · · · · · · · · · ·

Puppy and Good Manners classes are only the beginning of your training journey; once you "graduate," it is not the time to stop attending classes.

When Jazz and I began our first obedience class, I was still trying to control much of his behavior. Even though trainers were teaching me how to reinforce his conduct, I still wasn't making a connection with him. Though I am not sure exactly when I let go of trying to control Jazz and simply "trusted" him instead, that moment was when I began to feel a connection with him and when our training experience became fun for both of us. I became more relaxed, and he was happier because of it. With our newfound connection, I saw positive results from my training, and Jazz displayed pride in acquiring behaviors that pleased me.

My experience in this obedience class with Jazz was quite different from the one I attended with my first Portuguese water dog, Breezer, many years ago. In our first class, the instructor took the leash of a small dog and held him in the air until he stopped yelping; in fact, he almost stopped breathing. Both the owner and the rest of us in the class were horrified. My gut tightened and I told myself I would not let her do that to my dog. The instructor actually didn't repeat that action with any other dog in the class, but it was nonetheless disconcerting that she felt it was okay to do even once.

The important takeaway from this illustration is that dogs are helpless in these situations, and they need us to protect them, not inflict pain on them in the name of training. The owner of that dog who sat there feeling appalled was no different from me or others who are novices and first-time human parents to dogs. We often blindly trust the trainer to know what is best for our dog because we simply don't know any better.

Years ago, many trainers and human parents of dogs believed these negative techniques were the right methods to use. Even one of my friends who has been a dog trainer for many years says she shudders at some of the things we did to dogs in the past in the name of training. But with so much easily accessible information about dogs today through books and the Internet, there's no reason we shouldn't be educating ourselves. And now that we know *positive* not *negative* techniques are the norm, we must use that knowledge to guide us.

Once you've gone through obedience class with your dog, there's nothing that says you can't go through it again if you want to. I took Obedience I (One) two times with Jazz, not because he or I failed, but because it was an option to retake it, and I wanted to continue to learn the basic obedience behaviors in a structured environment.

A trainer friend of mine takes her own dogs to class, which elicits surprise from her friends who ask, "Why do you take your dogs to obedience classes when you can teach your dogs yourself?" She tells them that she not only likes the structure of the training process, but that her dogs enjoy the socialization to other dogs and humans they receive by being in the class environment.

While there are usually three levels of obedience classes offered, one and two are geared toward the average pet parent, and three is geared more toward people who are interested in obedience competitions. If you're a pet owner interested in further learning, however, you're welcome to take all the levels you wish.

When we completed obedience classes, we went on to Canine Good Citizen Class, which is a perfect opportunity to polish and finesse the obedience behaviors you've already learned. This is also great preparation for dogs who will be doing Animal Assisted Therapy. A dog who has obtained his Canine Good Citizen Certification is one who has proven he is successfully trained in the basic behaviors, making him a dog with good manners. It is a realistic and attainable goal for all dogs and a wonderful accomplishment.

· · · · · · · · · · · · · · · · · Leash Training · · · · · · · · · · · · · · · · ·

One of the most significant – and often one of the most challenging – activities you'll teach your dog is walking on a leash. One reason it presents such a challenge is that our dogs move faster than we do. Another is that they love being outside and become excited being on a walk, and many dogs like to spend much of the time sniffing and marking. Yet another is that along with intriguing smells, dogs encounter numerous distractions on a walk, such as other people and dogs; cyclists, runners, or roller bladers; cars and trucks; and squirrels or other critters. This all contributes to making the process of learning to heel challenging for a dog and the trainer.

Choosing Appropriate Equipment

One of the things that concerned me most when I was training my dogs to walk on a leash was their tendency to pull. Jazz is a strong dog, and he can easily pull me behind him and choke himself with his buckle collar in the process. Because pulling and choking is a common problem for most dogs when you are training them to walk on a leash, not to mention that it can be harmful to both you and your dog, a Gentle Leader® is an excellent tool.

As my dogs did not like having their head held with the leash constrain of the Gentle Leader® (most dogs don't, but many dogs adjust well to it), I began walking my dogs on the leash attached to the buckle collar. But in my case, Jazz still continued to pull a lot, so I found a harness that solved our problem. (Easy Walk® and SENSE-ation® are two brands among others you can try).

The benefit of the Easy Walk® harness I use is that it connects the leash at the front of the dog's chest, keeping him from being able to pull. Harnesses that connect the leash on the back of the dog, in contrast, actually teach the dog to pull. While this may be desirable for sled- or weight-pulling dogs to help better distribute their weight, it is not ideal when teaching a dog to walk on a leash. With a front-connecting leash, you have control of their body and can gently direct your dog without much tension on the leash at all.

My dogs wear this harness daily and our walks are very enjoyable, especially because they are not choking themselves and their strength is not pulling my arms out of joint. This is not such an issue with smaller dogs, but all dogs have the instinct to pull, so the front-connecting harness works well for all breeds.

The use of this type of harness also eliminates the need to use a harsh collar. Before I had the understanding I have now, a trainer convinced me to use a prong collar on Jazz when he was young. Despite the discomfort of it, however, he pulled a lot on the leash. After only a short time, I realized that he was stopping and sitting still to let the pain of the prongs digging in his neck wear off. Once I knew I was causing him distress this way, I immediately stopped using that collar and moved to the harness, which changed life for the better for both of us.

When it comes to collars, you want to choose a "friendly" style for your dog, one that doesn't create pain and is compatible with positive training techniques. Because my dogs have hair not fur, for example, even a flat collar will cut their hair. As such, I use a rolled collar that works well. Pet store personnel or your veterinarian can usually provide good guidance in choosing an appropriate style for your particular breed.

The next piece of equipment you'll need to purchase is a leash. With my first dog, Breezer, I bought a retractable lead for three reasons:

- It seemed everyone else was using it.

- I thought it would give my dog more room to explore and he would like that.

- I did not know of any better alternatives.

Now, however, I use a six-foot lead. While it undoubtedly offers greater benefits, I still see the majority of people walking their dogs on retractable leads, likely because they simply aren't aware that there's a better choice. Despite their widespread use, I have numerous concerns about utilizing retractable leads for everyday walks.

1. The retractable lead is very long, and if the pet parent is not watching closely, the dog can run into the street, get tangled in brush, or even lunge at another dog. The pet parent on the other end of the lead may have to travel a fair distance to get to their dog, which happens either after he has experienced a neck jerk in pulling as far as the lead will go, or the pet parent has tried to stop him by locking the lead and creating a neck and head jerk. These jerks can be harmful to the dog, and I see pet parents creating these frequently with this type of lead, even in close proximity. Because this is the only way you can control a dog's movement from any distance on this lead, and because repetition of these jerks can harm the dog, I don't recommend them.

2.   If the pet parent tries to grab the extended lead itself, it can cause burns to their skin or hand, not to mention that an arm or leg can get tangled in the lead, with severe bruising, breaks, or in extreme cases, amputation as a result.

3.   Because this lead can only teach a dog to pull, he will always be pulling away from you, rarely, if ever, walking alongside you enjoying your company on the walk.

4.   The handle to this lead is large and awkward to hang onto, and if you lose your grip, it can fall. As a result, your dog will likely walk or run off, with you unable to catch up. If you drop it in close proximity to your dog, the loud noise could frighten him. Depending on the dog, this could create anxiety about being attached to this lead in the future.

5.   When greeting other dogs on this lead, it easily becomes tangled with the leads of others. Even if you hold your dogs close and keep the leads short, the retractable lead is much more difficult to manipulate and often overlaps with others.

For all these reasons, I prefer the use of a six-foot lead for walking my dogs. In addition to the enhanced safety, I can also communicate much easier with my dogs because they are within reach at all times; I can ask them for a specific behavior and they will hear me. Also, because they are close enough to me, they can attune to my body language and the tone of my voice, feeling any tension and emotion from me through the lead.

If you have two dogs (or more) and always walk them together like I do, you will likely benefit from the lead I use, which is ideal for us. It has one loop handle, and both leads attach to the link at the handle, while the other end of each lead attaches to the harness of each dog. When we are walking, I only have to hold one loop handle in one hand, which keeps my other hand free to manage both leads as I need to. For example, when one dog is going to the bathroom, I can hold the other dog back at a comfortable distance.

I often see pet parents walking two dogs with each on a separate retractable lead, pulling and jerking on the leads a lot, which appears difficult to manage. The equipment we use, on the other hand, provides safety and comfort for the dogs and me, allowing us to enjoy our walks together.

The final equipment, so to speak, is an abundance of treats. You will need to reinforce your dog with frequent rewards in the progression of the walking/training experience, so if you're not wearing clothing with ample pockets, you may find a treat pouch that attaches to your waist helpful.

Now that you have the suitable equipment, you can begin training your dog to walk nicely on a leash. If you can, engage a trainer to guide you in this process, and above all, be patient. Take small steps, keeping your walking/training sessions brief in the beginning. As this activity can be taxing for you and your dog, you may have to find another form of exercise until you have mastered learning to walk on a lead. If you find your dog experiences issues on a lead, perhaps in feeling confined or behaving with agitation, know it is not uncommon. An experienced trainer can coach you through this, and as you positively train and reinforce your dog on this journey, you'll be able to increase your walking time. Remember also to set aside enough time for the training session, as you don't want to feel pressed to be somewhere else while you are with your dog in a training experience. Most of all, enjoy being with your dog and have fun!

· · · · · · · · · · · · · · · · · Crate Training · · · · · · · · · · · · · · · ·

I remember when I got Breezer, the breeder suggested to me that I "crate train" him. Not knowing what this meant, the term itself didn't sound good to me, but being the uninformed pet parent I was, I decided to pursue it. Luckily for me, this was something I did easily and favorably with Breezer.

Crate Training is essentially teaching your dog – in a positive way – to become comfortable being in a semi-confined space. Not only is it beneficial for traveling, but also in keeping your dog in a restricted space when you are away for short periods. It is also a space he can call his own, similar to having his own room within your home environment.

When purchasing a crate, you want to heed the following guidelines:

- The crate needs to be large enough for your dog to stand and turn around in, but not too much bigger than that. Your dog should feel the security of the four sides, but also move comfortably within. The crate needs to be large enough for your dog through all growth stages of his life. This may mean purchasing more than one crate or purchasing a crate with dividers to accommodate the different stages of growth.

- In choosing material – from hard wire to soft fabric – consider what will be the most practical for your dog and the crate's use.

- Almost all crates are portable, but some are more portable than others. As such, decide where in your house you will keep it. (We have a two-story house, so I have crates upstairs and downstairs. I also have crates that fold up easily for travel to dog events and human events.)

- If you're unsure which type to purchase, your vet or trainer can give you guidance in purchasing the crate most suitable for your dog and your needs.

- Remember to make the crate a cozy space – when dogs need time to themselves, they can go to their crate. In our home, for example, when I don't know where Jazz is, I always find him in his crate. Dogs need a space to call their own, somewhere just for them where no one else can bother them. For Jazz and Jive their crates are positive places, and the doors are always open so they can go in and out at their discretion.

While crates are a valuable resource and definitely have their benefits, I can't emphasize enough that they should never be abused.

When crate training a puppy, or even an older dog, be sure to never leave her in a crate any longer than she can hold her bladder or bowels. Here are some guidelines for keeping your puppy in her new crate:

Age Maximum	Time in Crate
8–10 weeks	30–60 minutes
11–14 weeks	1–3 hours
15–16 weeks	3–4 hours
17+ weeks	4–5 hours

Remember that crate training itself is a short-term endeavor; once house-training is complete, your dog will no longer need to be in the crate as much. When a dog becomes "trustworthy," meaning she can be trusted to be in the home without restriction, she will no longer need to be crated, even when you are away.

My dogs have long been trustworthy, and when I leave they have access to the house. If I will be gone for more than six hours, though, I hire a pet sitter to come and let the dogs out and walk them. This works well for us, but if you're still using a crate while you're away, it is important to be responsible and mindful of the length of time your dog will be in it. If you will be gone longer than the guidelines I gave earlier, you should hire a pet sitter or have a friend, neighbor, or family member come over to let your dog outside and walk him. This is not only the humane thing to do for your dog, it will give you peace of mind as well.

Again, I want to emphasize that using a crate must never be abused. There are two definite don'ts regarding crate training:

- Do not use a crate to contain your dog simply because he's a nuisance and requires attention. A puppy or young dog can sometimes be annoying and exhausting, but it's unfair and negligent to lock him up, rather than provide the training he needs.

- Do not put your dog in his crate to punish him. If you do, he'll understandably come to dislike the crate.

While it's fine to use the crate sparingly as a time-out place, your dog should have many more pleasant experiences than not with his crate to counteract any possible unpleasant associations. It goes without saying that in order for your dog to be comfortable in a crate, you as the pet parent need to introduce it in a positive way and with patience – and I always recommend using treats as reinforcement!

Crate training is covered in Puppy Class, but you can also learn from a trainer or attend a class anytime if you have an older dog. Regardless of a dog's age, the benefits of crate training are numerous.

Traveling with a Crate

Using a crate in a car is the safest way for dogs to travel, so you need to ensure that your car can accommodate it. When I bought my latest car, I told the salesman I needed a car for two dogs and a grandchild. If, however, your car is too small for the crate that fits your dog appropriately, there are seat belts for dogs that work very well and should always be used when transporting them by car.

Using a Crate for Safety Reasons

When we go to public events at parks, I put my dogs on leads, but I also bring crates should there be any reason to contain them for their own protection. Anytime there are numerous dogs present, crates are a safety measure for the dogs and for the humans. When we go to dog events, for example, every participant has a crate for their dog. This ensures that chaos doesn't ensue and that harm comes to no one.

If you have a dog with a lot of anxiety, and you have tried to make the crate a positive experience – even gradually – without success, it may simply be something that won't work for your dog. While professional trainers may be able to help you and your dog overcome this, if this doesn't prove true for you, respecting your dog's abilities is just as important as maintaining his safety. There is no sense in forcing a dog to do something that doesn't work for him, no matter how gentle and patient you are. After trying all options to crate train your dog, at the end of the day, loving your dog and having fun with him is what is most important.

· · · · · · · Integrating Training into Daily Activities · · · · · · ·

As we discussed in Chapter Nine, it is critical to keep your dog's new learned behaviors alive on a daily basis from the beginning of your training journey together. When your dog masters a new behavior, you can ask her to display it during your day-to-day activity. As a reminder, here are a few examples you can follow:

- When you give her a treat simply because you want to, make her earn the treat with a "sit."

- When you go to sit on the sofa and she is in your spot, ask her to get "off." Then, if you want to ask her to join you, invite her back with "paws up," or whichever word or phrase you have designated for this.

- If she is sniffing something you don't want her to sniff, ask her to "leave it."

- If you are in another room, call your dog to "come."

By incorporating these learned behaviors into your day-to-day activities, your dog will feel integrated into your life. He will appreciate that you are communicating with him and asking him to do the job of being a well-mannered dog. Not only is a trained dog a lot of fun to live with, he feels a sense of purpose and is able to live comfortably in our human world.

*G*OING *A*BOVE AND *B*EYOND

Properly trained, a man can be dog's best friend.
— COREY FORD

Once your dog has mastered basic behaviors and you are now a team who enjoys learning and working together, you can pursue additional activities. In addition to teaching your dog tricks, which is a wonderful way of promoting ongoing mental and physical learning for him, there are also several canine sport, Animal Assisted Therapy, and service options to explore. Many people think sports for dogs are great, but don't think they have the time to devote to anything like competition sports. Granted, it does take a lot of dedication and devotion to both the dog and the sport; however, competition has rewards for both the pet parent and the dog. Factors you'll want to consider include cost, type of sport, and whether to compete or just have fun with the sport.

· · · · · · · · · Exploring Involvement in Sports · · · · · · · · ·

Although it requires a level of commitment to participate in structured sports for dogs, the benefits are numerous. Not only does it provide great exercise for all involved, it also creates a further bonding experience for you, your dog, and your family. If you have interest in this type of activity, there are two ways you can participate: in general classes of varying levels, or in actual competitive dog sports.

Sports for Fun

When I first considered sports options with Jazz and Jive, I knew I wasn't able to commit to a given sport with the goal of competing in it. Fortunately for me, there was a training school in my area that offered the opportunity to simply "explore" classes in different sports.

We began with "Exploring Agility" and had so much fun learning about the sport that we moved up to the intermediate level. As the school offered the option to take classes and learn just for fun, we didn't have to commit to training classes for organized competition events. Enjoying a sport without feeling the pressure to compete is the optimal choice for many pet parents, so if this is your goal as well, this type of program will be perfect for you.

Although the Agility classes were a positive learning experience for all of us, we realized with time that it wasn't necessarily our sport; finding one we all enjoy has been a journey of trial and learning, much like exposing your human child to various sports. After dabbling in Agility, for example, we tried Conformation and Freestyle, neither of which were quite our thing either. But then we enrolled in K9 Nose Work, and I knew we'd found *our* sport. Both Jazz and Jive love it and so do I, and what's great is that it's a sport you can participate in either for fun or for competition. We've been attending classes regularly for over two years now.

While we enjoyed exploring different sports options and our bond grew even stronger as we learned more about each other, it was important to discover what worked best for us as a team. Good teams in dog sports work like one unit, and if you truly love a sport, learning the skills should feel less like work and more like fun.

For me, I discovered that K9 Nose Work resonated strongly because it allowed me to learn about my dogs' basic instinct of smell. Other trainings, like obedience, tend to guide dogs *away* from sniffing, which is in contrast to their instinct. In K9 Nose Work, however, we teach dogs to use their noses as they were intended – watching my dogs enhance their natural instinct to sniff and work with their noses is actually quite exciting.

While we began the sport to participate just for fun, I later learned that the competition was different from others in that only you and your dog are present in the room with the judge and steward. This type of competition was more suited to me, so while my intention was not to compete because I didn't think I would be comfortable in that venue, we are now preparing for it. Though it remains to be seen how far we'll go in actual competition, we will remain in our weekly classes because the experience is so positive for all of us.

If you're not familiar with K9 Nose Work, it encompasses teaching dogs to search in four areas: interiors, exteriors, vehicles, and containers. When we compete, we add to the search one of the three odors dogs need to recognize: birch, clove, and anise. (This has actually put a twist in my holiday baking because I used to bake anise pizzelle cookies; now, however, I have to make *almond* pizzelle cookies. The aroma of anise throughout the house would drive the dogs crazy, prompting them to look for the animal hide with the anise scent, which would frustrate them and possibly negatively influence their search experience in the sport.)

A perk of this sport is that any dog or handler can participate as there is no speed or heavy exertion involved. We even have a dog who is blind in our class.

The three things I love most about K9 Nose Work are:

1. As a handler, you must learn to read your dog's body language and get to know how she works with her nose to "alert the find" at the end of the search. This builds your bond with your dog quickly as you become a team working side by side.

2. This is a sport you can do in the house on days that are too cold, hot, or rainy. On nice days, you can do searches in your backyard, on your deck, or anywhere you can safely be with your dog.

3. As noted before, competition is only you and your dog; no other dogs or competitors are in the room. For me this makes it very personal. It also eliminates "winning" against others and feels more like collaboration than competition.

Because Jazz, Jive, and I love doing K9 Nose Work together, we look forward to the times we can fit it into our schedule; it gives us all a sense of purpose and a fun time together, which is a win-win experience.

Competitive Sports

If taking your participation in sports with your dog to a competitive level interests you, you will need to consider three key requirements: the commitment of time, the purchasing of equipment, and the investment of money.

Time

Depending on the sport you choose, classes usually run for an hour to an hour and a half and last five to six weeks for each level. Each successive level prepares you and your dog for competition at varying stages. The weekly commitment you can expect ranges from two to five hours or more, which will fluctuate based on the time you dedicate to practicing at home, as well as your travel time.

Equipment

Naturally, different sports will require various types of equipment. For example, in K9 Nose Work you need a crate for your dog and a leash to guide her on searches. If you choose to compete, you will need the essential oils of anise, clove, and birch that denote the odor for the search, as well as containers to hold the scent if you wish to practice outside the classroom. Be sure to inquire at the outset what, if any, equipment is necessary to participate in your chosen sport and if it falls within your budget.

Money

Most structured activities require some level of financial investment, and canine sports are no different. Here are some of the expenses you can expect:

- The cost of each course, which is typically $125–$190 for six weeks

- Varying costs for the specific sport's equipment, as well as crates for transport

- Travel to competitions

- Hotel accommodations

- Competition fees

Groups and Team Dynamics

National organizations abound that host competitive events across the U.S, and other countries have similar organizations and events as well. You will find that those who are involved are quite serious about their activities, so if you're a person devoted to your dog and a specific sport, and you love the sport as much as your dog does, competition will suit you well. Be aware, however, that you don't want to pursue a sport you enjoy but that your dog doesn't. I have seen duos like this, and they are difficult to watch in action. It is much like watching a parent at a hockey or soccer game cheering for their child, and the child is performing solely to please the parent, not because he loves the sport. As such, it is important to separate your motives from your dog's ability and desire for the sport and find an activity you both enjoy.

Sports for Specific Breeds

As dogs are bred with different skills, sports exist that enhance these inbred abilities. For example, water trials are suited to breeds like the Portuguese water dog; earth dog competition is suited to terrier breeds. Lure courses are great for sight hounds like greyhounds, while competitions like Obedience, Rally, and Conformation are inclusive of all dogs. Certain sports, like Agility, require speed and litheness, which may not work well for larger breeds. That does not mean, however, that a dog of a muscular breed could not participate in Agility and even enjoy it. What's important is to experiment, to find a sport that's a good match for your particular dog, and to make sure your dog is safe and enjoying it.

The Benefits of Canine Sports

A few of the numerous benefits you and your dog will receive from sports participation are:

- Your dog stays active and keeps in good physical health and condition.

- You are partnering together and building a bond while getting to know each other.

- Your dog receives mental challenge and stimulation.

- Your dog has a purpose and a job, as well as something exciting to look forward to.

- The ongoing training helps your dog develop trustworthy behaviors.

- You and your dog have FUN and enjoy being together, which is what having a dog in your life is all about!

When considering a sport, whether for fun or for competition, the following are some of the better-known sports you can pursue:

- Agility
- Canine Freestyle
- Conformation
- Disc (Frisbee) Dogs
- Dock Diving
- Earth Dog Trials
- Flyball
- Herding Trials

- Hunting
- K9 Nose Work
- Lure Coursing
- Obedience
- Rally
- Tracking
- Water Trials
- Weight Pulling

A friend of mine once asked me how I knew Jazz and Jive loved doing
K9 Nose Work as a sport. The answer was easy: not only did both dogs
become excited when we arrived in the parking lot for class, their tails
wagged, they vocalized happy sounds, and they couldn't wait to have
their turn searching. Even when we practice at home, they get excited
when I bring the bag of search items down from the cupboard, and both
go immediately into their crates where they know to wait for their turn to
search. When we tried other sports, they enjoyed them but not to the
same level as K9 Nose Work. I, too, excelled more at K9 Nose Work than
I did in other sports, making it a win-win for us!

Do keep in mind that whether you do a sport for fun or for competition,
your dog is now an athlete, and athletes can get injuries. As they need to be
cared for appropriately, inquire if your veterinarian specializes in the treatment of certain sport-related injuries; if not, seek out one who does. Dog
athletes need to be kept in shape to be able to perform the sport-required
skills with minimal risk for injury.

If your schedule and budget allow for it, I highly encourage you to explore
canine sport options that may appeal to you and your dog. Remember, you
can observe classes to see what is actually involved before you commit. When
you match what you know about your dog's interest and abilities to specific
sports, you may just find one you both fall in love with, enabling you to experience all the wonderful benefits of participating in a canine sport together.

· · · · · · · · · · · · Being of Service Through · · · · · · · · · · · · Animal Assisted Therapy

Sports are a wonderful outlet for dogs, but if sports aren't your thing, or
you simply want to explore additional activities for you and your dog together,

there are several ways to participate on the service side. Jazz and Jive, for example, are active in K9 Nose Work as well as in Animal Assisted Therapy, in which animals are used for therapeutic purposes. This involves working with a professional, setting goals, and documenting progress. Jazz, Jive, and I receive goals and lesson plans for our sessions with clients, and we discuss how we will incorporate the dog's behavior for the client's benefit.

. . . .

Note that this work is different from Animal Assisted Activity, which does not require documentation and goals, and involves visiting clients in a nursing home or hospice, where patients pet the dog and she provides comfort by being present. Note also that therapy dogs are not the same as service dogs. There are no federal laws to comply with in Animal Assisted Therapy, and the dogs are not allowed to accompany their handler anywhere in public other than the designated area for therapy visits.

. . . .

Two of the better-known organizations that provide training specifically for Animal Assisted Therapy are Pet Partners and Therapy Dogs International. The training is usually twelve weeks long and involves classroom lecture and time working with your dog. This leads up to the final evaluation you and your dog must pass to become qualified to perform Animal Assisted Therapy. Prior training, such as basic obedience and Canine Good Citizen Certification, is required on certain levels and is highly valuable before beginning a program of this nature.

A significant benefit of working with one of the aforementioned organizations is that qualified teams are covered with liability insurance. Another is their structured renewal process. For example, Pet Partners requires both the dog and the handler to demonstrate comprehensive skills used in therapy work, as well as requiring a vet exam and keeping all information about the dog current every two years.

This type of service work does require a financial investment — $150 to $200 or more the first year for the training, manual, and vet exam — but if it fits into your budget, the benefits far outweigh the cost.

Jazz, Jive, and I have been working with children in hospital and trauma preschool settings for over six years. Because each dog has his or her own personality, and no two dogs perform therapy work in the same way, dogs are matched up with the needs of the client. For example, Jazz is very interactive and likes playing games like ball and find-it, which involves the child hiding a dog toy and Jazz finding it. Jive, in contrast, will play some games, but she prefers to be petted and to cuddle with the child or adult. Both dogs have an enormously positive impact on the clients we see.

If Animal Assisted Therapy is something you wish to consider, here are some details about my experience to help you decide if the commitment and expectations will be suited to you and your dog.

I became certified and began doing this work with Jazz over six years ago. For the first three years, we provided service weekly at a children's hospital, where we enjoyed the engagement with a diverse population. We also participated in one-on-one sessions with a child and the occupational therapist, and I quickly learned that both Jazz and I enjoyed the one-on-one sessions the most.

In one memorable session, the occupational therapist was working with a child who needed to develop some motor skills and finger dexterity. She asked the child to color on a piece of paper with any color in any way she wanted to. Jazz lay next to the little girl, who was on her stomach on the floor. When she finished her drawing and picked it up to show it to Jazz, he turned his head and licked her on the cheek. She was elated.

While many people would see that lick as random, handlers who work with animals in therapy settings know this kind of interaction between humans and animals is not random in the least. Rather, it is the result of a definite connection between the child or adult and the animal. Seeing this connection and the gift it provides to both parties is what makes the work extraordinary for me personally.

Two years ago, I trained with Jive and she became certified in AAT, but I learned pretty fast that bringing both dogs did not work out so well – the kind of therapy work we do is best suited for one dog at a time. For this reason, we rotate sessions so that Jazz comes one week and Jive comes the next. The staff at the facility enthusiastically support the work we do and enjoy the dogs as much as the clients. In fact, a staff person will often ask to pet Jazz or Jive and say, "I need a Jazz moment" or "I need a Jive moment."

As their jobs can be quite stressful, staff members sometimes need time with a therapy dog as much as a client – a few minutes petting a dog can do wonders.

Jazz, Jive, and I currently visit two facilities, one of which is a trauma preschool program for children eighteen months to five years of age. These are highly stressed kids, most of whom are in child protection. In this environment, we work in one-on-one sessions with a psychologist and a child, where we integrate the dog's therapeutic behavior into the psychologist's lesson plan.

While it's regrettable that any child would need to be in a facility like this, the improvements we're able to make with these children are impressive. For one example, Jazz worked with a four-year-old boy who chose not to speak as a way to deal with the stress in his life. When he was with Jazz, however, he became comfortable speaking. He asked Jazz to find toys and catch a ball, and he would take Jazz on walks in the building. The psychologist and I were always supervising the interaction, of course, but having Jazz as a part of his therapy aided his ability to speak and make other progress, such as increased self-confidence. The psychologist documented that the boy improved at a faster pace with Jazz being involved than he would have otherwise.

Another inspiring story was with a three-year-old girl we worked with who had a lot of anxiety as well as many fears, one of which was a fear of dogs. When we introduced her to Jazz, the psychologist held her at a safe distance, and Jazz did an interesting thing. He lay down and instinctively looked away from her as the psychologist read a story. Initially, the child was frightened to be near Jazz at all, but as time passed, she relaxed more and more. Shortly after the book was completed, she agreed to throw a ball for Jazz and quickly became confident in this. Then she began hiding toys for Jazz to find. Soon after that, she was able to pet Jazz. By the end of the half-hour session, she was smiling and couldn't get enough activity with Jazz. When the psychologist took her back to the classroom, the first thing the little girl did was run to her teacher and say, "Miss Helen, I'm not scared of Jazz anymore!" Watching a three-year-old confront and work through her fear in a half hour was incredible to observe.

The second facility we visit is one for adults with developmental disabilities. The clients have various levels of learning abilities – some have
physical limitations, are nonverbal, or are in wheelchairs. As Jazz and Jive
have been trained to work around items such as wheelchairs, beds, chairs,
and tables, as well as in the presence of elevators, loud noises, and lots of
people, they are quite comfortable in this environment and look forward to
spending time there.

During my first visit to the facility with Jive, about ten people were
seated in a circle. Most were on chairs, but two were in wheelchairs. One
was upset because he had finished his snack and wanted more, so he left
his chair and crawled onto the floor, making loud noises to express his
unhappiness. The staff were concerned that the loud noise was frightening
Jive, but I was watching her closely and she wasn't demonstrating any
stress at all; in fact, she was pulling toward the man. I cautiously guided her
to him, and despite his verbal venting, Jive approached him and licked him
on the cheek. At that moment, he became calm and smiled, ceasing his
tantrum and engaging Jive with eye contact. Seeming to be concerned for
him, Jive stayed by his side. Soon after, he returned to his chair and participated in the session.

Although I had concerns in that situation, I could sense that Jive was
feeling confident. In trusting her and carefully allowing her to lead an interaction where I could keep her protected, Jive impressed me with her first
therapy visit. She continues to do great work, as does Jazz.

Another client at this same facility always asks for "Jazz Dog." She is
impulsive and talks loudly, but she has learned to use her indoor voice and
to sit patiently while waiting her turn to pet Jazz in a therapy session.
Everyone at the facility agrees that she has accomplished this significant
behavior change more quickly than would have occurred without Jazz's
involvement.

Observing my dogs performing Animal Assisted Therapy is an opportunity
to see how attuned they are to varied human emotions, body language, and
tone of voice. Dogs and humans exchange an emission of oxytocin, which is

the hormone that makes us feel love and happy to be with someone. Research now confirms that this is a factor that makes Animal Assisted Therapy such a positive and successful experience for all involved. And dogs aren't the only animals who perform AAT – horses, guinea pigs, cockatoos, and many others have proven to make a positive difference.

Therapy work with your dog is certainly a rewarding experience. But even more, it is an opportunity to observe the fascinating connection between a dog and a human being – and with consistently favorable results. It is yet another example of how much value our wonderful dogs bring to the human experience.

· · · · · · · · · · · The Role of the Service Dog · · · · · · · · · · ·

Service dogs are a testament to the intelligence, stamina, love, and skill that dogs possess. They essentially become the "ability" for a person with a "disability."

Service dogs and Animal Assisted Therapy dogs have different training and therefore different responsibilities. The Americans with Disabilities Act of 2010 defines service animals as "any dog that is individually trained to do work or perform tasks for the benefit of an individual with a disability, including a physical, sensory, psychiatric, intellectual, or other mental disability." When people with limited ability can add a trained service dog to their life experience, their lives are transformed and they form a true partnership between their dogs and themselves as humans.

As you might expect, service dog training often begins in puppyhood and can take from six months to a year or longer, depending on the type of disability the dog is being trained for. Two key elements of the training are mitigating the specific disability and behaving appropriately in public to avoid being removed. After being trained by a professional program, the dog will then require an ample amount of time for direct training with the person with the disability. Last, for the partnership to be successful, the dog and handler must be able to build a strong and trusting bond.

Some training programs will also assess your family dog to see if he or she may be helpful to you if you have or develop a limitation of your own. For example, I was given a hearing loss diagnosis, and so I inquired about how Jazz might be able to "become" my ears by hearing things like the phone or doorbell if I was ever unable to. Though this never developed into a problem for me (and I suspect, in fact, that it was a misdiagnosis), they determined he would be a good candidate. The result? If I would ever need a dog to provide assistance for me, it is good to know there are many resources available.

When I see a service dog at work, I marvel at the relationship between the human and the dog, at how they exemplify the partnership that can exist with all pet parents and dogs. However, there is growing concern that some people put service dog vests on their dogs to falsely "qualify" them to enter shops and restaurants. For people with true service dogs, this is understandably unsettling. As service dogs are highly trained and have worked hard to become the partner for their human with a disability, bringing a dog who is not sufficiently trained to a public place can have a negative result, especially for the dog.

Some people with dogs who do Animal Assisted Therapy work also believe they can take their dogs to public areas other than the facility they do therapy in. This, however, is not acceptable. Not only is misrepresenting a dog who is not a trained service dog a deception and not in alignment with the Disabilities Act, only certified service dogs are allowed in public venues that are accessed by their human with the disability.

As I've said, if we want our dogs to be able to go with us to more public venues, we need to earn that right by training them, ensuring both dogs and people are safe at all times. Whether your dog is a house pet to love, a trained Animal Assisted Therapy dog, or a certified service dog, he needs to have the manners and socially acceptable behaviors that will allow him to be in public venues comfortably. Only then will we be able to enjoy the company of our canine companions wherever we go. I can't say enough that training our dogs consistently throughout their lifetime is the greatest way to show our love for them.

· · · · · · · · · · · · **PART FOUR** · · · · · · · · · · · ·

Some Final Thoughts

· ·

WHEN THINGS DON'T WORK OUT

There is no faith which has never yet been broken,
except that of a truly faithful dog.
— KONRAD LORENZ

hen we bring a dog into our lives, it is often at a time of stability in our human relationships. But that same stability can be at risk when unpredictable events occur, such as an economic downturn, losing a job, changing family circumstances, going through a breakup or divorce, or experiencing illness or loss.

We can't foresee when the economy will take a hit and shifts will occur. As I mentioned in a previous chapter, many people could not take their dogs with them to new living locations during the housing foreclosures in the recent recession. Others could not afford to care for their dog after losing their home, and the dogs were found left alone in the vacated house.

Similarly, when a breadwinner loses his or her job, it typically causes financial stress on the entire family. Priorities change, and that can mean making tough decisions; feeding and caring for a pet may simply be too much for their new budget to handle. Though no pet parent wants to face this grueling situation, sometimes it means that it's necessary to find a new home for the dog.

Another challenge people sometimes face after falling in love with their dog is when one or more persons in the family develop allergies. While some will attempt to deal with those allergies with medication, more often than not, they decide they simply cannot keep the dog.

I have a friend who had had a dog in his life since he was a child. When he met his wife, he and his beautiful golden retriever of two years were bonded and very happy together. His fiancée had extreme allergies to dogs, and he therefore made the heartrending decision to rehome his dog. He found a great home for him, but his voice is still sad when he talks about this unfortunate event.

A new baby can also shift the family dynamic when a dog is a family member before the birth of the first human child. If there is no preparation for the dog in this new situation, when the baby comes home, it can be stressful for the family. As a result, they may feel the need to find a new home for the dog, or worse, surrender him to a shelter.

If you encounter the need to give up your dog, regardless of the situation, please consider the following before you simply drop your dog off or believe a shelter is your only choice:

- Ask neighbors or relatives if they might be interested in giving your dog a loving home, or if they know anyone who might.

- Email everyone on your list with a photo and honest description of your dog and his personality to see if anyone you know might be a willing candidate as his new pet parent.

- If you purchased a specific breed, the breeder may have in your contract that they will take your dog and rehome her.

- Seek a breed-specific rescue group to help you rehome your dog. If you don't have a specific breed, there are rescue groups for mixed breeds as well.

- Use social media to promote a fundraiser to help keep your dog or to advertise your wish to rehome a dog. Be sure, however, to investigate all potential pet parents carefully, and never make a decision without meeting in a safe place in person.

While all of these circumstances present unwanted challenges, perhaps the most volatile is when two people split up or divorce, especially when there are children and pets in the family. Statistically, half the marriages in the United States end in divorce; if a couple isn't married, they must merely negotiate custody as amicably as they can. Either way, the ending of a once-happy relationship is a stressful experience regardless of the circumstances. Dealing with emotions as well as splitting assets and belongings can exacerbate an already painful time, but breaking up an entire family brings added stress and heartbreak. No one wants to have to let go of their children, and when pets are considered as much a part of the family as the children – or when they are the "only" children – it becomes even more complicated.

Not too long ago, the family pet was viewed in a divorce as property to be divided, along with the house, possessions, and finances. In fact "property" is how the law defines a pet. But according to the Animal Legal Defense Fund (ALDF):

> Although animals are considered property in the eyes of the law at this time, some courts are beginning to recognize that one's relationship with this particular form of property known as the family cat, dog, bird etc., is much different from one's relationship with other forms of property such as your couch, your watch, or your coffee pot.

The courts are now considering pet custody as being influenced by some of the following key factors (these have been worded to reflect families with dogs):

- Who is the person who takes the dog to the veterinarian?

- Who trains the dog?

- Who walks and feeds the dog?

- Who is the dog bonded to?

- Who can best afford the cost of maintaining the dog?

The answers to these questions help determine who receives custody.

I have a friend who recently married. Her husband is divorced, and as he and his ex-wife both wanted time with their dog, they have shared custody, not unlike they might have with a child. As a result, they rotate time with their dog every other month.

Dogs need consistency, and in stressful experiences like a divorce, it is not uncommon to observe changed behaviors in your dog, such as not eating or having accidents in the house. Those who settle on a shared custody arrangement need to therefore provide as much consistency as possible to help their dog make the transition to his new living situation. Dogs need support to adjust under these circumstances just as human family members do.

Sometimes during a divorce, people will try to hurt each other, using the children or pets as weapons. This of course only creates more pain for everyone, so agreeing on as many points as possible before the final divorce can reduce some stress. Being in harmony on things like which partner will pay for what costs, who will be in charge of taking the dog to the veterinarian, and ensuring you are both feeding him a similar diet and maintaining exercise will motivate you to keep your dog's best interest at heart.

While the separation of a family is undeniably distressing, perhaps one of the most heartrending is when elderly friends and relatives become ill or reach a point where they are unable to care for their pet.

Several years ago, an elderly relative of ours had a stroke. Not only did she have a dog she loved dearly, but she had always been the person who took care of everyone else's dogs when they went on vacations. Sadly, besides being left unable to care for her dog, her stroke left her with no long-term memory. She still loved dogs, but she didn't remember she had one of her own. Although this was devastating to all who knew her and to her dog, another family member happily adopted him, and our relative was never aware that she lost a dog she loved.

While this story had a happy ending for the dog, these types of life events happen all the time, often without such a favorable outcome. When people are ill or become incapable of caring for their pets, the pets are frequently surrendered to an animal shelter. You now know, however, that this is not the only option.

If, despite your best attempt at all the options listed on pages 146–147 you're unsuccessful in finding a home for the dog, the animal shelter may be your only choice. Not only is it traumatizing for a dog to have to be surrendered, it is equally difficult for the pet parent to part with her. If, however, surrender is the only option, seek a no-kill shelter if at all possible. There your dog will have a better chance of being rehomed; in other shelters, the outcome is too often euthanasia. Above all, remember that there are options and that most people will want to help you and your dog however they can – all you have to do is ask.

Saying Good-Bye

True friends leave pawprints on our hearts.
– Unknown

Nearly everyone who has a dog in his or her life will tell you that the relationship is special and that it is different from other relationships with humans. Because dogs live in the moment at all times and have a way of keeping us present with life, the sense of connection with a dog is unique. When I am spending intentional focused time with my dogs, for example, I am in that moment with them. Most people I know, myself included, do not live in the moment as well as dogs do. We try, but it seems more difficult for humans to accomplish this with much consistency.

Living in the moment is a constant way of being for dogs. Not only do they bring us to where they are, but they pass no judgment or complaint toward us no matter how we treat them, which is why it breaks my heart when I see any dog treated poorly – or simply ignored.

Some say our dogs find *us* and are here to teach us something we need to learn on our life journey, such as patience, unconditional love, and how to have fun. When I was struggling to successfully manage Jazz's exuberant puppy energy, a dear friend, who happens to be one of the best dog trainers I know, said, "Jazz is a lot of dog, and he is here to teach you something."

That statement made a big impact on me, and it's true that I have learned many things in my relationship with Jazz. The most valuable is the joy I feel when I am simply with him in the moment and let go of everything else happening in my life. Being in his presence and completely in the moment is healing and rejuvenating for me. If you have a dog, you have likely experienced the same.

Dogs are not perfect beings, but they do bring a sense of joy and acceptance to our shared lives with them. Their companionship is unlike any other I have experienced. During my corporate career, for example, I traveled a lot. When I was away from home on a business trip, I always missed my husband and son, but what I missed most of all was the constant companionship of my dog. Whenever I share this experience with others in conversation, someone always emphatically agrees and shares their own experience of missing their dog. When people struggle to find words to describe how they feel about their dogs, I believe what they are trying to explain is that they feel a mutual acceptance of each other without judgment.

Now that I travel less, when I'm working in my home office at my computer, one dog is lying at my feet and the other is on the floor behind my chair. Merely knowing they are there is relaxing for me. I love being around their energy, and my home feels empty when they are not in it. It is devastating to imagine the day when they are gone forever.

Saying good-bye to our dogs is always heartbreaking, but because dogs have much shorter life spans than humans, it is something we have to know and accept when we bring them into our lives. One unknown author said:

> "When humans come into the world, they try to live a good life and learn to live in love and compassion and courage. Dogs come into the world already knowing how to do this and that is why they are here for such a short time."

On one of my recent walks with Jazz and Jive, we met another family walking their dog and stopped for the dogs to greet each other (after determining all were friendly, of course). Their dog was older and moving slowly, and Jazz and Jive were very gentle with him, not sniffing him as they normally would. As we were talking, the woman was dabbing her eyes with a tissue. She told me this was the last walk for their dog, that the vet was coming to their home later that afternoon to put him down. I was so moved by the love she had for her dog that I shared my tears with her. Her husband and daughter were heartbroken as well. They were saying good-bye to a dog who was a member of their family for fourteen years, and they all wanted to be with him on his last walk, as well as in their home when he said good-bye. Although I wished I could have offered more support for the family than crying myself, I think they knew my tears were heartfelt ... my empathy was certainly real.

I remember when we as a family said good-bye to Breezer, my husband positioned himself at an angle so that his face would be the last thing Breezer saw as he was leaving. It was one of those life experiences each of us will remember always. I was also deeply touched by how our veterinarian made it a respectful and loving experience for Breezer and for us, and I will always feel gratitude toward her for that.

Everyone has a special connection with their dog, and finding out he or she is ill or may not have much time left is crushing. But one woman I read about recently, after receiving a terminal illness diagnosis for her dog, did something thoughtful — she created a bucket list for him to accomplish before he passed away. Among other things, she made sure he ran free in a meadow and ate an ice cream cone. What a wonderful celebration of life!

Saying good-bye to someone we love, including our dogs, is only one part of the journey. When we are committed to a relationship, we see it through from the beginning to the end, and the end is often the hardest. While letting go is incredibly painful, it's important to remember how much your dog loves you and that he would be there for you if you were the first to leave. So be there for him when he needs you most of all.

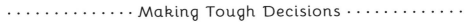
· · · · · · · · · · · · Making Tough Decisions · · · · · · · · · · · ·

While we would all love it if our dogs simply fell asleep when their time came, life with dogs often requires us to make some tough decisions.

Oftentimes the remaining quality of life and level of pain influence a decision sooner than we had expected, and a pet parent instinctively knows when this time is at hand. It takes love and courage to be there for our dogs; this is a time they need us the most. And while we understandably struggle, I believe a dog knows how hard it is for their pet parent to see them declining and to let them go, because it is just as hard for the dog. Human or canine, saying good-bye is the hardest part of loving.

At the end of Breezer's life, he was full of cancerous tumors and was unable to swallow. We cried for days, and I put a scrapbook together with pictures of his life journey, which was very healing for me. When the time came, we had him cremated and were so grief-stricken over losing him that we simply put the ashes away to deal with at a later time. After about three years, I suggested to my husband that it seemed time to return Breezer's ashes to his backyard. We both felt confident we could do this, but when we opened the container and sprinkled the ashes, both my husband and I instantly began crying. Even after such a long period, our sadness overtook us. While we were fortunate to have each other, as well as the photo album of memories and many other people we could talk with who supported us in our loss, it was nonetheless painful to experience that loss all over again.

It is difficult for many people to express grief at the loss of a loved one or friend, and it can be equally challenging for them to feel comfortable supporting other people through their grief. When someone has to say good-bye to their dog, it is not uncommon to receive little to no support from others. A common reaction is, "It's just a dog. You'll get another one and all will be well again." Few people understand the depth of pain over the loss of a pet, yet everyone I know who has lost one has experienced significant sadness for a long time. It is not unlike the loss of anyone in your life whom you love.

One of the most helpful things you can do for yourself when you are grieving is to talk about it. But you must choose people who understand your loss and will listen without judgment. If you have no one in your personal life who can empathize with you, your veterinarian and the staff at the vet clinic will be supportive. If you're able to surround yourself with people who love dogs and can relate to your loss, it can be quite comforting. Most of all, let yourself heal over time. Our dogs leave paw prints on our hearts that last forever, and it is important for us to allow ourselves the time to grieve and listen to our hearts as we remember them. One day, as occurred for us, you'll be healed enough to bring another pet into your life, if you so choose.

Another thing to consider is how your other dogs will feel when one passes away. Anyone who has multiple dogs and has lost one of them will tell you that the living dogs expressed sadness over the loss of their friend.

A regular acquaintance of ours who has always walked her two cocker spaniels over the past eight or nine years recently had only one dog with her. She told me the other dog had passed away and that her remaining dog was very sad. She described how her dog seemed beside herself and lost, like she didn't know what to do without her best friend.

I have friends who have two dogs, and when one is reaching senior years, they intentionally adopt a third dog to bond with, not only for themselves, but for the dog who will be left behind when the senior dog passes on. If this isn't an option for you, it is crucial to recognize that your remaining dog is grieving as you are. Allow your dog to see and say good-bye to the dog who has passed so that he will know where his bonded friend is and not go through the house looking for him. Talk to him about how you both miss your friend and companion. Give yourself and your dog time to grieve and heal. Throughout the grieving period and beyond, enjoy the wonderful times with your loving companion who is still with you.

Today, there are numerous ways you can honor the loss of your beloved dog – urns for ashes, gravestones, garden stones, and wind chimes can all be engraved to honor their memory. While your dog is healthy and growing up with you, take pictures and videos when you can to capture the moments that will someday be a lasting memory. Enjoying life with your dog is a gift, and finding a way to capture many of those moments to enjoy when your dog is gone is another gift you can give yourself.

LAST NIGHT

I stood by your bed last night, I came to have a peep.
I could see that you were crying, you found it hard to sleep.

I whined to you softly as you brushed away a tear,
"It's me, I haven't left you, I'm well, I'm fine, I'm here."

I was close to you at breakfast, I watched you pour the tea,
You were thinking of the many times your hands reached down to me.

I was with you at the shops today, your arms were getting sore.
I longed to take your parcels, I wish I could do more.

I was with you at my grave today, you tend it with such care.
I want to reassure you that I'm not lying there.

I walked with you toward the house as you fumbled for your key.
I gently put my paw on you, I smiled and said, "It's me."

You looked so very tired and sank into a chair.
I tried so hard to let you know that I was standing there.

It's possible for me to be so near you every day.
To say to you with certainty, "I never went away."

You sat there very quietly, then smiled, I think you knew ...
In the stillness of that evening, I was very close to you.

The day is over ... I smile and watch you yawning
and say, "good-night, God bless, I'll see you in the morning."

And when the time is right for you to cross the brief divide,
I'll rush across to greet you and we'll stand side by side.

I have so many things to show you, there is so much for you to see.
Be patient, live your journey out ... then come home to be with me.

—Author Unknown

Hope for Dogs and Humans

*The greatness of a nation and its progress can be judged
by the way its animals are treated.*
— Mahatma Gandhi

Hope is the belief that change can happen. Making the connection from loving our dogs to intentionally becoming more informed about them is significant. Someone once said that knowledge is power, and it's true that the information we have about any situation directly influences the decisions we make. The more knowledge we have about our dogs, the more meaningful our bond becomes with them. That not only means that the more we educate ourselves about our dogs, the greater our relationship grows, but also that we will make more informed decisions regarding our dogs' welfare.

Becoming educated has a direct impact on today's dog overpopulation problem. As more and more pet parents become aware and informed, and in turn share that information with other pet parents, the ripple effect will be unstoppable. Pet parents will view training their dogs as a primary responsibility, and the number of dogs surrendered to shelters will decrease, while the quality of life for dogs and the humans who love them will positively increase. Trainers, veterinarians, breeders, and pet parents must be partners and advocates in this venture.

·············· Engage and Self-Educate ············

As a pet parent, we have numerous resources available to us so we can make a positive difference for dogs. Accessing information from books, websites, and articles from dog-educated friends and associations like the Humane Society of the United States (HSUS), the American Society for the Prevention of Cruelty to Animals (ASPCA), and other dog-related organizations is free and easy to do. There is a huge population of dog-welfare advocates, and you can easily be one of them by simply being a responsible pet parent. Educating ourselves is a great beginning to being the change we want to see in the world for our dogs.

Tʜᴇ Tᴏᴘ Tᴇɴ Qᴜᴀʟɪᴛɪᴇꜱ ᴏꜰ ᴀ Sᴜᴘᴇʀ Pᴇᴛ Pᴀʀᴇɴᴛ

1. Is clear about why they have a dog in their life and commits to being a pet parent for better or worse and for the lifetime of their dog.

2. Respects and understands the differences and similarities between a canine pet and a human child and embraces all as family members.

3. Researches and plans for the type of dog who will realistically fit into their lifestyle.

4. Is able to make the commitment of responsibility, time, and money necessary to maintain the daily needs of a dog for his or her entire life.

5. Provides lifelong socialization and training experiences for their dog.

6. Makes sure the dog has an annual wellness exam with a veterinarian and provides ongoing medical care, including spaying or neutering, as well as providing ongoing dental hygiene by brushing their dog's teeth regularly.

7. Provides their dog with a purpose and a job such as engaging in a dog-related sport or regular activities, or performing service, rescue, or therapy work.

8. Provides healthy nutrition and is informed about nutritional options.

9. Provides both physical and mental exercise for their dog.

10. Has FUN with their dog and builds their bond by spending time together.

Your strong relationship with your dog will be evident to friends, and even strangers, who see you interact with her. People will be inclined to ask you questions – every time I'm with other people and their dogs, discussion is almost guaranteed to happen. Why? Because people love their dogs and enjoy talking about them. They often want to learn more, and what better way to do that than through another pet parent? When you engage in these discussions, you have an opportunity to share your experience and knowledge in a heartfelt way that will in turn help another pet parent and their dog.

· · · · · · · · · · · · · · · · Volunteering · · · · · · · · · · · · · · · · ·

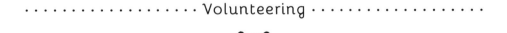

Another means to self-educate is to volunteer – whether working in a humane animal shelter, fostering dogs for rescue groups, or participating in therapy programs, it can be a life-changing experience.

Assisting Shelters

Shelters are always in need of volunteers and typically welcome all the assistance they are offered. People I know who walk, feed, or play with dogs at shelters learn a great deal and know they are making a difference for their welfare. Many shelters also have fundraiser walks, which are opportunities to walk with your dog for a good cause, as well as a chance to meet others who share your desire to make a difference in the animal world.

Foster Parenting

Being a foster parent is a short-term situation where you care for and train a dog until he is placed in a forever home. Shelters and rescue groups are always in need of reliable, caring foster homes. I know some truly remarkable individuals who do this repeatedly, some of whom commit to a two-year program to keep and train a puppy who will be a service dog for someone with a disability. After the two-year time frame, as hard as it is to give the puppy up for his next phase of training, they say it is even more gratifying to know the kind of wonderful work he will eventually be doing to make someone's life complete, filling it with love and companionship.

Therapy and Service

While we discussed therapeutic and service work in detail in Chapter Eleven, it's worth mentioning again that it's a wonderful way to positively engage your dog and help others while doing it. The volunteer work in Animal Assisted Therapy I do with Jazz and Jive makes a significant impact on everyone involved; there's nothing better than making a true difference for dogs and for people.

If you have any spare time, I wholeheartedly encourage you to seek out volunteer opportunities in your community. Dogs have so much to give, and when we engage with them – on any level – we each benefit greatly from that experience.

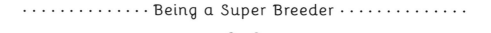

· · · · · · · · · · · · · Being a Super Breeder · · · · · · · · · · · ·

A responsible breeder has incredible influence in educating a potential pet parent. A breeder with passion and love for their breed operates with ethics in their practices, putting the welfare of the breed before the monetary gain. This commitment to their values is evident when they interview and select pet parents for their puppies. A responsible breeder is truly a mentor and coach for either a new or experienced pet parent, educating them about their breed and about how to spot irresponsible breeders. In addition to operating in an ethical manner, responsible breeders should offer support in the following two critical ways:

- Educating the pet parent on all aspects of caring for and being responsible for their new puppy/dog, as well as taking on the role of ongoing coach, which means being available initially and then continuing to provide guidance and information over the years.

- Being a model of an accountable breeder and educating others about responsible practices, allowing pet parents to know how to discern a responsible breeder from an irresponsible one.

Breeders are essential to propagating healthy breeds that have been around for decades, or even centuries. As every breed was initially bred for a purpose and always to help mankind in some manner, it is incumbent upon a breeder to perform their responsibility of reproduction ethically. With these ethics at the core of breeding along with legislation to support the practice, dogs will only be bred to preserve the breed and it will be much more difficult for people to engage in overbreeding primarily for profit.

· · · · · · · · · Veterinarians as Powerful Educators · · · · · · · · ·

I am fortunate to have a veterinarian I not only like and admire, but who is one of the best educators I have ever known. It is my hope that you have — or will be able to find — one equally wonderful. Every time I bring my dogs to see her, I learn something new, and she always explains why she recommends a particular protocol. For example, I once brought Jive in because she was barely eating and was throwing up what little she had eaten. This was completely out of character for her, so my vet recommended blood work along with an x-ray to make sure there was no blockage. After the procedures, my vet showed me the x-ray and explained its findings and the blood work in detail, which revealed that Jive had a GI upset. I was relieved to learn there was no obstruction or other serious problem, and she recovered within thirty-six hours.

I encourage you to find, build, and sustain a comfortable, respectful relationship with your veterinarian that will grow with your dog. Being diligent about wellness visits and keeping your vet informed about concerns you have will help you both know your dog and his needs throughout his lifetime.

I know veterinarians want to help pet parents take the best possible care of their dogs, so I encourage them to think of themselves as powerful educators; when they do, we become even more empowered as pet parents, which is a win-win for everyone, especially our dogs.

· · · · · · · · Trainers as Educators, Role Models · · · · · · · · and Communicators

It is not uncommon for us to look to trainers to have all the answers, trusting they will know just what to tell us to solve our problems with our dogs. As such, trainers are in a position to be hugely influential educators. While we discussed the importance of vetting a trainer well in Chapters Nine and Ten, and that certainly still holds true, most trainers are sincerely committed to making the world a better place for dogs. They all too often see dogs who are not experiencing an ideal life situation due to a lack of training; their goal is to therefore provide that training so that pet parents can not only make life better for their dogs, but for themselves as well.

Trainers often have their own dogs and model being positive pet parents, even sometimes incorporating their dog as a demo in the training session. This gives parents in the class the opportunity to see the relationship between the dog and trainer in action – education through modeling is powerful.

A trainer with good people skills, as well as one who implements positive techniques, is ideal. An effective trainer communicates well that the training is for the pet parent and guides them to be successful with their dog. As you can imagine, a trainer's job is challenging; convincing a pet parent to spend time training their dog is no small feat, and yet motivating them to commit to it is crucial. As we've said before but is worth repeating: if dogs are to successfully remain with their humans and not be surrendered to a shelter when they become too difficult to live with, the commitment to training needs to change dramatically, and an excellent trainer who communicates that is a vital inspiring force.

Another way trainers can make a positive difference is when exposing a pet parent to training for the first time. Because that initial experience influences the pet parent's attitude about training, and because first-time pet parents can be vulnerable and impressionable, trainers have a responsibility to set a positive tone in all interaction and training techniques from the start. Once on a positive path to training, a pet parent is likely to relate to and train their dog in a way that is respectful and is a positive experience for both the dog and themselves. When this occurs, it contributes to dogs remaining happily in their human homes and to keeping another dog from becoming part of the pet overpopulation problem.

TOP TEN QUALITIES OF A SUPER TRAINER

1. Is clear about why they want to work with people and dogs in a training capacity.

2. Enjoys working with people as well as with dogs.

3. Understands how critical it is to provide training and coaching for the human pet parent.

4. Implements only positive training techniques, never using negative tools such as prong collars, shock collars, or any form of dominance training.

5. Has formal training with a respected professional program.

6. Makes the training experience fun for the human and the dog.

7. Views themselves as a communicator, educator, and trainer.

8. Remains current on training techniques by attending professional conferences and participating in ongoing training for their own development.

9. Models positive training techniques with their own dogs, if applicable.

10. Conducts themselves in a professional manner.

. . . .

"Never doubt that a small group of thoughtful, committed citizens can change the world; indeed, it's the only thing that ever has."
−Margaret Mead

. . . .

All concerned persons and all who have the power to effect change can make a huge difference for our dogs and the humans who love them, but it is a community effort. Veterinarians, trainers, breeders, advocacy organizations, Humane Society shelters, rescue groups, and legislation are each in a position to educate and better life for dogs today. And while all of these factors are valuable, I believe the most powerful agent for change is the pet parent. An educated pet parent who has trained their dog with love and positive training techniques, and has made a lifelong commitment to him, is the most powerful support a dog can have. When you model your positive relationship with your dog and educate others about dogs when the opportunity presents itself, it is invaluable. Not only are those things key to solving our dog overpopulation problem, they are vital to enhancing the natural and necessary love and respect between humans and animals that can only lend to a harmonious existence for all.

TEN COMMANDMENTS FOR A RESPONSIBLE PET PARENT

1. My life is likely to last ten to fifteen years. Any separation from you will be very painful.

2. Give me time to understand what you want of me.

3. Place your trust in me. It is crucial for my well-being.

4. Don't be angry with me for long and don't lock me up as punishment. You have your work, your friends, your entertainment. I only have you.

5. Talk to me. Even if I don't understand your words, I understand your voice when it is speaking to me.

6. Be aware that however you treat me, I'll never forget it.

7. Before you hit me, remember that I have teeth that could easily crush the bones in your hand, but I choose not to bite you.

8. Before you scold me for being lazy or uncooperative, ask yourself if something might be bothering me. Perhaps I am not getting the right food, I've been out in the sun too long, or my heart may be getting old and weak.

9. Take care of me when I get old. You, too, will grow old.

10. Go with me on difficult journeys. Never say, "I can't bear to watch it," or "let it happen in my absence." Everything is easier for me if you are there. Remember, I love you.

—author unknown

RESOURCES

Books

Brown, Steve. *See Spot Live Longer*. Creekobear Press, 2004.

Brown, Steve and Beth Taylor. *Unlocking the Canine Ancestral Diet*. Wentachee: Dogwise Publishing, 2010.

Coren, Stanley. *How to Speak Dog*. New York: Free Press, 2003.

Donaldson, Jean. *The Culture Clash*. Berkeley: James & Kenneth Publishers, 1996.

Dunbar, Ian. *Before and After Getting Your Puppy*. Novato: New World Library, 2004.

Dunbar, Ian. *How to Teach a New Dog Old Tricks*. Berkeley: James & Kenneth Publishers, 1996.

Grandin, Temple and Catherine Johnson. *Animals Make Us Human*. New York: Mariner Books, 2010.

Grandin, Temple and Catherine Johnson. *Animals in Translation*. 2005. Reprint, New York: Harvest Books, 2006.

Hall, Lee. *On Their Own Terms: Bringing Animal-Rights Philosophy Down to Earth*. Darien: Nectar Bat Press, 2010.

Kay, Nancy, MD. *Speaking for Spot: Be the Advocate Your Dog Needs to Live a Happy, Healthy, Longer Life*. 2011.

Korpi, Sid. *Good Grief: Finding Peace After Pet Loss*. Minneapolis: Healy House Books, 2009.

McConnell, Patricia B. *For the Love of a Dog*. New York: Ballantine Books, 2007.

McConnell, Patricia B. *The Other End of the Leash*. New York: Ballantine Books, 2003.

Monks of New Skete, The. *Divine Canine*. New York: Hyperion Books, 2007.

Rugaas, Turid. *On Talking Terms with Dogs: Calming Signals*. 1997. Reprint, Wentachee: Dogwise Publishing, 2005.

Sundance, Kyra and Chalcy. *101 Dog Tricks*. Gloucester: Quayside Publishing Group, 2007.

Taylor, Beth and Karen Shaw Becker. *Real Food for Healthy Dogs & Cats*. USA: Natural Pet Productions, 2011.

Williams, Marta. *Learning Their Language*. Novato: New World Library, 2003.

Zak, Paul J. *The Moral Molecule*. 2012. Reprint, London: Corgi Books, 2013.

Websites

American College of Veterinary Behaviorists
dacvb.org

American Kennel Club
akc.org

American Veterinary Dental College
avdc.org/periodontaldisease

Americans with Disabilities Act 2010
ada.gov/2010_regs.htm

Animal Legal Defense Fund
aldf.org

ASPCA (American Society for the Prevention of Cruelty to Animals)
aspca.org

Association of Professional Dog Trainers
apdt.com

Dr. Karen Becker, D.V.M.
healthypets.mercola.com

Certified Applied Animal Behaviorists
certifiedanimalbehaviorist.com

Certified Council for Professional Dog Trainers
ccpdt.org

Dr. Stanley Coren
stanleycoren.com

Dog Food Advisor
dogfoodadvisor.com

Dog puzzles
activedogtoys.com
nina-ottosson.com

Dogster
dogster.com

Humane Society of the United States
humanesociety.org

Intermountain Therapy Animals
therapyanimals.org

Journal of Applied Animal Welfare Science (JAAWS)
tandfonline.com/toc/haaw20/current

National Association of K9 Scent Work
nacsw.net

National Council on Pet Population Study and Policy
sawanetwork.org/national-pet-council.html

Pet Partners (Pet Assisted Therapy training)
petpartners.org

Susan Thixton
truthaboutpetfood.com

Therapy Dogs International
tdi-dog.org

United Kennel Club
ukcdogs.com

References

List of Foods Dogs Should Not Eat
humanesociety.org/animals/resources/tips/
foods_poisonous_to_pets.html

Number of AKC Breeds and Total Number of Breeds in the World
numberof.net/number-of-akc-breeds/

Responsible Breeder Criteria
akc.org/press-center/facts-stats/responsible-breeders/

Socialization for Dogs Checklist
aspca.org/pet-care/virtual-pet-behaviorist/dog-behavior/socializing-
your-puppy

Research

American Psychological Association. "Dogs' Intelligence On Par With Two-
year-old Human, Canine Researcher Says." ScienceDaily.
www.sciencedaily.com/releases/2009/08/090810025241.htm (accessed
October 7, 2015).

ASPCA. About Us, Pet Statistics. "Facts about U.S. Animal Shelters."
www.aspca.org/about-us/faq/pet-statistics (accessed October 7, 2015).

ASPCA Professional. "Food Guarding: A Very Modifiable Behavior."
www.aspcapro.org/resource/saving-lives-adoption-programs-behavior-
enrichment-research-data/food-guarding-very (accessed October 19, 2015).

Drake, Justine. "Nutrition Lessons from Man's Best Friend: University
research shows that fresh, wholesome foods may be healthier for dogs than
processed kibble." PRNewswire.com. www.prnewswire.com/news-

releases/nutrition-lessons-from-mans-best-friend-university-research-shows-that-fresh-wholesome-foods-may-be-healthier-for-dogs-than-processed-kibble-261652391.html (accessed October 7, 2015).

Humane Society of the United States. "Animal Cruelty Facts and Statistics." HumaneSociety.org. www.humanesociety.org/issues/ abuse_neglect/ facts/animal_cruelty_facts_statistics.html (accessed October 7, 2015).

Zak, Paul J. "Can dogs and cats actually love?" TheAtlantic.com. www.theatlantic.com/health/archive/2014/04/does-your-dog-or-cat-actually-love-you/360784/ (accessed October 7, 2015).

Trainers

Jean Donaldson
academyfordogtrainers.com

Ian Dunbar
dogstardaily.com/blogger/4

Susan Hodsgon
whendogstalk.com

Patricia B. McDonnell
patriciamcconnell.com

Victoria Stilwell
positively.com

O

oatmeal, 68

Obama, Barack, 12

obedience class (*see* training)

older dogs, 80, 92

101 *Dalmatians*, 12

onions/onion powder, 65

P

peach pits, 65

Pet Partners, 135, 171

pet sitter(s), 35, 80, 81, 123

Portuguese water dog, 2, 3, 4, 5, 12, 13, 24, 25, 44, 58, 87, 116, 132

Portuguese Water Dog Club, 44

potato leaves, 65

preventive medications, 35

prong collar (*see* collars)

protein (*see* nutrition)

pumpkin, 67

puppy/puppies, 3, 4, 11, 12, 15, 32, 33, 43, 44, 47, 52–54, 55, 77, 92, 101, 107, 111, 114, 123, 151, 162, 163

puppy class (*see* training)

puppy college (*see* training)

puppy kindergarten (*see* training)

puppy mills, 45–46

puzzles, 81–82, 171

R

raisins, 65

Rally, 132, 133

rehome, 146, 147, 149

relationship

    development of, 2, 3, 4, 7, 8, 15, 17, 21, 26–29, 33, 41, 81, 90, 93, 100, 103, 107, 111, 141, 151, 159, 161, 164–165, 166

    with veterinarian, 58–60

rescue, 13, 17–18, 46, 111, 161

rescue group(s), 12, 20, 46, 47, 146, 161, 162, 166

retractable lead (*see* leashes)

rhubarb (leaves), 65

· · · · · · · · · ACKNOWLEDGMENTS · · · · · · · ·

I want to recognize the dogs and humans who have meant so much to me on my journey in the world of dogs.

My dear Breezer, I think of you nearly every day and thank you for your constant love. I know someday I will see you again and you will be wearing that goofy, wonderful smile you shared with everyone who knew you.

Jazz, you are my special boy and I can't begin to thank you for all I have learned about being in a bonded trusting relationship with a dog. Every day you do something to make me smile, and every day I feel our bond grows closer.

Jive, you are my special girl. You have taught me so much about how dogs each have their own personality and are true individuals. Your never-ending affection is a wonderful gift I enjoy and am grateful for. I feel our bond, too, grows with every day.

Sweet Tish, you showed concern for me always. You had such a fun disposition even though you didn't have much consistency in your life with me. You showed me lessons in loyalty I came to understand and appreciate much later.

To all the dogs I have had the pleasure of meeting and spending time with, thank you for being here with us humans. Thank you for being by our sides and for your desire to want to make our lives better with your presence. I am constantly impressed with the fact that you can hurt and maim a human with a bite of your strong teeth and jaws, yet unless trained to do so as our courageous police canines, or forced to bite to defend yourself, rarely do you act out toward us in that way. You want to be at our side and walk our journey with us; your loyalty and companionship is a gift. Thank you for all you do to teach us how to live a compassionate life, for that is what happens in a trusting bonded relationship between a dog and a human being.

My friends and family who walk on two legs, you have been my constant source of support and inspiration. My husband Jim, my son Brandon, my like-a-daughter Becky, and my two grandsons Dominic and Leo, thank you for always cheering me on and rooting for me to make my goals and dreams a reality. Our family is a priceless gift I am so grateful for. I appreciate each of you opening your hearts to Jazz and Jive and inviting them to be a vital part of our family life. We share an abundance of love.

My sisters Sally Lane and Kathy Birtzer, you are a never-ending source of support and joy in my life. Thank you for always being there for me with a hug and a smile.

I am blessed with friendships that have endured the test of time. To Pat Wall, Nancy Herbst, Kris Muyskens, Kathy Birtzer, and Christine Pepper, thank you for reading my book and giving testimonials to what you found helpful in my written words. Elaine Garley, thank you for joining my journey and giving your time and expertise to proofread my book. Thank you Kate An Hunter, for your generosity and friendship. When I needed a space to film, you offered your gorgeous backyard, which worked out perfectly. Nikki Aune, my friend, videographer, editor, longtime supporter, I couldn't have done my TV show or the promotional videos for the book without you. I love that our hearts and minds are in harmony when we work together, bringing our shared passion to life. Joshua Richard, my creative genius friend, you shared my visions and made them all a reality designing my website. I love your imagination and your kind, open heart. Thank you for sharing both with me. Laurie Erickson and Breana Voss, thank you for capturing the moment with my dogs and me so beautifully. Your photos hold those moments forever and for many to enjoy. Kathy Sparrow, my first editor, I am so grateful you took on the challenge of my first draft and guided me to a foundation for my book. And I want to thank Stacey Aaronson for her superb editing skills that brought my book to life. I believe we are connected at a creativity level of the soul. I can't imagine this book could have happened without your guidance and skills. We worked hard and somehow always enjoyed a laugh and delight in what we created. You have made this journey very special and memorable for me.

And to my friends and relatives who expressed support and eagerness to read my book, I thank you. It means a lot to know there is a network of people who value my contribution.

To everyone who has shared this journey with me, thank you for caring about our beloved dogs. Please never stop caring.

Woofs & Smiles!

*D*ONNA CHICONE is an author, animal advocate, entertainer, and pet parent – a joy and responsibility she takes very seriously.

After leaving a twenty-three-year career in corporate America, Donna began her quest to help make life better for dogs and the humans who love them. This led to the creation and hosting of the TV show, *The Dog Show with Jazz*, which ran for forty-eight episodes with her then sole Portuguese water dog as co-host. During the last year of the show, her second Portuguese water dog, Jive, joined them.

Committed to ensuring Jazz and Jive have a purpose, both are trained as Animal Assisted Therapy dogs and currently work with children aged two and a half to five in a trauma preschool setting, as well as in a facility for adults with developmental disabilities. To keep them mentally and physically challenged, both dogs also attend ongoing K9 Nose Work classes and compete in the sport as well.

Donna's advocacy for all animals is expressed in her lifestyle of eating a vegan diet and supporting efforts to end cruelty to farm and wild animals. Her passion for the welfare of dogs, as well as her desire to educate others that all animals are sentient beings who feel pain, fear, joy, and love, motivated her to write *Being a Super Pet Parent*. Her sincere wish is for every dog to be loved by a human who understands and embraces the commitment of having a dog in his or her life. When humans make this relatable connection with animals, they achieve a mutual respect for each other, whereby cruelty to animals has less opportunity to exist.

Donna lives with her husband in Minnesota where they enjoy spending time with their one son, his wife, and two grandsons.

jazzandjive.com

30264142R00114

Made in the USA
Middletown, DE
18 March 2016